maran
illustrated™

Computers

maranGraphics®

&

THOMSON™

COURSE TECHNOLOGY

Professional ■ Trade ■ Reference

MARAN ILLUSTRATED™ Computers Guided Tour™

© 2005 by maranGraphics Inc. All rights reserved. No part of this book may be reproduced or transmitted in any form or by any means, electronic, mechanical or otherwise, including by photocopying, recording, or by any storage or retrieval system without prior written permission from maranGraphics, except for the inclusion of brief quotations in a review.

Distributed in the U.S. and Canada by Thomson Course Technology PTR. For enquiries about Maran Illustrated™ books outside the U.S. and Canada, please contact maranGraphics at international@maran.com

For U.S. orders and customer service, please contact Thomson Course Technology at 1-800-354-9706. For Canadian orders, please contact Thomson Course Technology at 1-800-268-2222 or 416-752-9448.

ISBN: 1-59200-880-1

Library of Congress Catalog Card Number: 2005921021

Printed in Canada

05 06 07 08 09 TC 10 9 8 7 6 5 4 3 2 1

Trademarks

maranGraphics is a registered trademark of maranGraphics Inc. Maran Illustrated, the Maran Illustrated logos and any trade dress related to or associated with the contents or cover of this book are trademarks of maranGraphics Inc. and may not be used without written permission.

The Thomson Course Technology PTR logo is a trademark of Course Technology and may not be used without written permission.

All other trademarks are the property of their respective owners.

Permissions

KDE
KDE, K Desktop Environment and the KDE Logo are trademarks of KDE e. V.

Microsoft
© 2005 Microsoft Corporation. All rights reserved.

Smithsonian Institution
Copyright © 1996 Smithsonian Institution

CBS SportsLine
Copyright © 1996 SportsLine USA, Inc.
http://www.sportsline.com All rights reserved.

YAHOO!
Text and artwork copyright © 1996 by Yahoo! Inc. All rights reserved. YAHOO! and the YAHOO! logo are trademarks of YAHOO!, Inc.

AMD
AMD, the AMD ARROW logo, AMD Athlon, AMD Sempron, AMD Turion and combinations thereof, are trademarks of Advanced Micro Devices, Inc.

Other Permissions Granted:
CyberPatrol
Discovery Channel Online
Energy Star
Google
Intel
Linspire
Sunkist

Important

maranGraphics and Thomson Course Technology PTR cannot provide software support. Please contact the appropriate software manufacturer's technical support line or Web site for assistance.

maranGraphics and Thomson Course Technology PTR have attempted throughout this book to distinguish proprietary trademarks by following the capitalization style used by the source. However, we cannot attest to the accuracy of the style, and the use of a word or term in this book is not intended to affect the validity of any trademark.

Copies

Educational facilities, companies, and organizations located in the U.S. and Canada that are interested in multiple copies of this book should contact Thomson Course Technology PTR for quantity discount information. Training manuals, CD-ROMs, and portions of this book are also available individually or can be tailored for specific needs.

THOMSON

COURSE TECHNOLOGY
Professional ■ Trade ■ Reference

Thomson Course Technology PTR, a division of Thomson Course Technology 25 Thomson Place ■ Boston, MA 02210 ■ http://www.courseptr.com

maranGraphics®

maranGraphics Inc.
5755 Coopers Avenue
Mississauga, Ontario
L4Z 1R9
www.maran.com

maranGraphics is a family-run business.

At **maranGraphics**, we believe in producing great computer books– one book at a time.

Each maranGraphics book uses the award-winning communication process that we have been developing over the last 30 years. Using this process, we organize screen shots and text in a way that makes it easy for you to learn new concepts and tasks.

We spend hours deciding the best way to perform each task, so you don't have to! Our clear, easy-to-follow screen shots and instructions walk you through each task from beginning to end.

We want to thank you for purchasing what we feel are the best books money can buy. We hope you enjoy using this book as much as we enjoyed creating it!

Sincerely,

The Maran Family

We would love to hear from you! Send your comments and feedback about our books to family@maran.com

Please visit us on the Web at:
www.maran.com

Credits

Authors:
Ruth Maran
Kelleigh Johnson

Technical Consultant & Post Production:
Robert Maran

Project Manager & Editor:
Judy Maran

Editor:
Jill Maran Dutfield

Proofreader:
Jennifer March

Layout Artist & Illustrator:
Richard Hung

Illustrator:
Russ Marini

Indexer:
Kelleigh Johnson

**President,
Thomson Course Technology:**
David R. West

**Senior Vice President of
Business Development,
Thomson Course Technology:**
Andy Shafran

**Publisher and General Manager,
Thomson Course Technology PTR:**
Stacy L. Hiquet

**Associate Director of Marketing,
Thomson Course Technology PTR:**
Sarah O'Donnell

**National Sales Manager,
Thomson Course Technology PTR:**
Amy Merrill

**Manager of Editorial Services,
Thomson Course Technology PTR:**
Heather Talbot

Acknowledgments

Thanks to the dedicated staff of maranGraphics, including
Richard Hung, Kelleigh Johnson, Wanda Lawrie, Jill Maran,
Judy Maran, Robert Maran, Ruth Maran, Jennifer March,
Russ Marini and Raquel Scott.

Finally, to Richard Maran who originated the easy-to-use
graphic format of this guide. Thank you for your
inspiration and guidance.

Table of Contents

CHAPTER 3

PROCESSING

CHAPTER 4

STORAGE DEVICES

CHAPTER 5

SOFTWARE

CHAPTER 6

OPERATING SYSTEMS

Table of Contents

CHAPTER 11

E-MAIL AND INSTANT MESSAGING

CHAPTER 10

THE INTERNET AND THE WORLD WIDE WEB

CHAPTER 1

INTRODUCTION TO COMPUTERS

Do you want to learn more about your computer? This chapter is the place to start.

HARDWARE AND SOFTWARE

Hardware and software are the two basic parts of a computer system.

HARDWARE

Hardware is any part of a computer system that you can see or touch.

Peripheral Device

A peripheral device is any piece of hardware attached to a computer, such as a printer, keyboard or mouse.

SOFTWARE

Software is a set of electronic instructions that tell a computer what to do. You cannot see or touch software, but you can see and touch the packaging the software comes in. There are two types of software—application software and operating system software.

Application Software

Application software allows you to accomplish specific tasks, such as composing documents and creating and editing images. Popular application software includes Microsoft Word and Adobe Photoshop.

Operating System Software

Operating system software controls the overall activity of a computer. Most new computers come with the Windows XP operating system software.

There are many ways to get help with your computer system.

DOCUMENTATION

Hardware and software should include documentation that tells you how to set up and use the product. Many software packages also come with a built-in help feature that you can access while using the software. You can also check local book stores for manuals with detailed, step-by-step instructions.

CONSULT THE EXPERTS

If you have questions about setting up or using new hardware or software, you can try contacting the store where you purchased the product. You can also contact the manufacturer of the product for help or look on the manufacturer's Web site to see if a solution is provided for the problem you are encountering. Lastly, you can visit a local computer repair shop or check your telephone book to find a computer expert who can come to your home to fix the problem.

CLASSES

Colleges and computer training centers offer courses that can teach you how computers work and how to use specific software. You can also check your local library, community center and computer stores for computer classes.

A computer collects, processes, stores and outputs information.

INPUT

An input device allows you to communicate with a computer. You can use input devices to enter information and issue commands. A keyboard, mouse, scanner, microphone and joystick are input devices.

PROCESS

The Central Processing Unit (CPU) is the main chip in a computer. The CPU processes instructions, performs calculations and manages the flow of information through a computer system. The CPU communicates with input, output and storage devices to perform tasks.

STORE

A storage device stores information. Popular examples of storage devices include a hard drive, a recordable CD drive, a recordable DVD drive and a multi-card reader.

OUTPUT

An output device allows a computer to communicate with you. A monitor, printer and speakers are output devices. These devices display information on a screen, create printed copies and generate sound.

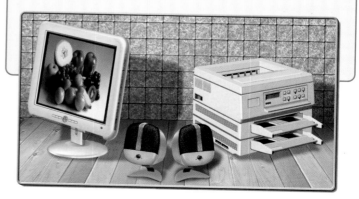

> Bytes are used to measure the amount of information a device can store.

Byte

One byte is one character. A character can be a number, letter or symbol. One byte consists of eight bits (binary digits). A bit is the smallest unit of information a computer can process.

Kilobyte (KB)

One kilobyte is approximately equal to one thousand characters or one page of text.

Megabyte (MB)

One megabyte is approximately equal to one million characters or one book.

Gigabyte (GB)

One gigabyte is approximately equal to one billion characters or a shelf of books in a library.

Terabyte (TB)

One terabyte is approximately equal to one trillion characters or an entire library of books.

TYPES OF COMPUTERS

There are several types of computers.

PC (PERSONAL COMPUTER)

A PC is a computer designed to be set up and used in one location, usually on a desk. PCs are commonly thought of as computers running the Windows operating system and are found in most businesses and homes. Popular manufacturers of PCs include Dell and Hewlett-Packard.

MACINTOSH

Macintosh computers, made by Apple Computer, are found in some homes and businesses and are very popular in the graphics, publishing, music and film industries. The Macintosh computer was the first popular personal computer that offered a graphical display.

NOTEBOOK

A notebook computer is a small, lightweight computer that you can easily transport. All the components of a notebook, including the keyboard, pointing device, speakers and screen, are built into one unit. Notebooks come with a rechargeable battery which allows you to use the computer when no electrical outlets are available, making notebooks ideal for frequent travelers.

HANDHELD

Handheld computers, also known as Personal Digital Assistants (PDAs), are lightweight computers that are small enough to carry in your hand. Handheld computers usually include an electronic pen, called a stylus, that you use to select items on a small, touch-sensitive screen.

Some handheld computers also include a keyboard. You can use a handheld computer to perform most of the same tasks as other types of computers, such as word processing and Web browsing. Handheld computers use rechargeable batteries as their power source.

A typical computer system consists of several parts.

Monitor

A monitor is a device that displays text and images generated by a computer.

Printer

A printer is a device that produces a paper copy of documents you create on a computer.

Computer Case

A computer case contains the major components of a computer.

Cable or DSL Modem

A cable or DSL (Digital Subscriber Line) modem is a device that allows you to connect a computer to a high-speed Internet connection.

Speakers

Speakers are devices that play sound generated by a computer.

Keyboard

A keyboard is a device that allows you to type information and instructions into a computer.

Mouse

A mouse is a handheld device that allows you to select and move items on the screen.

INSIDE A COMPUTER

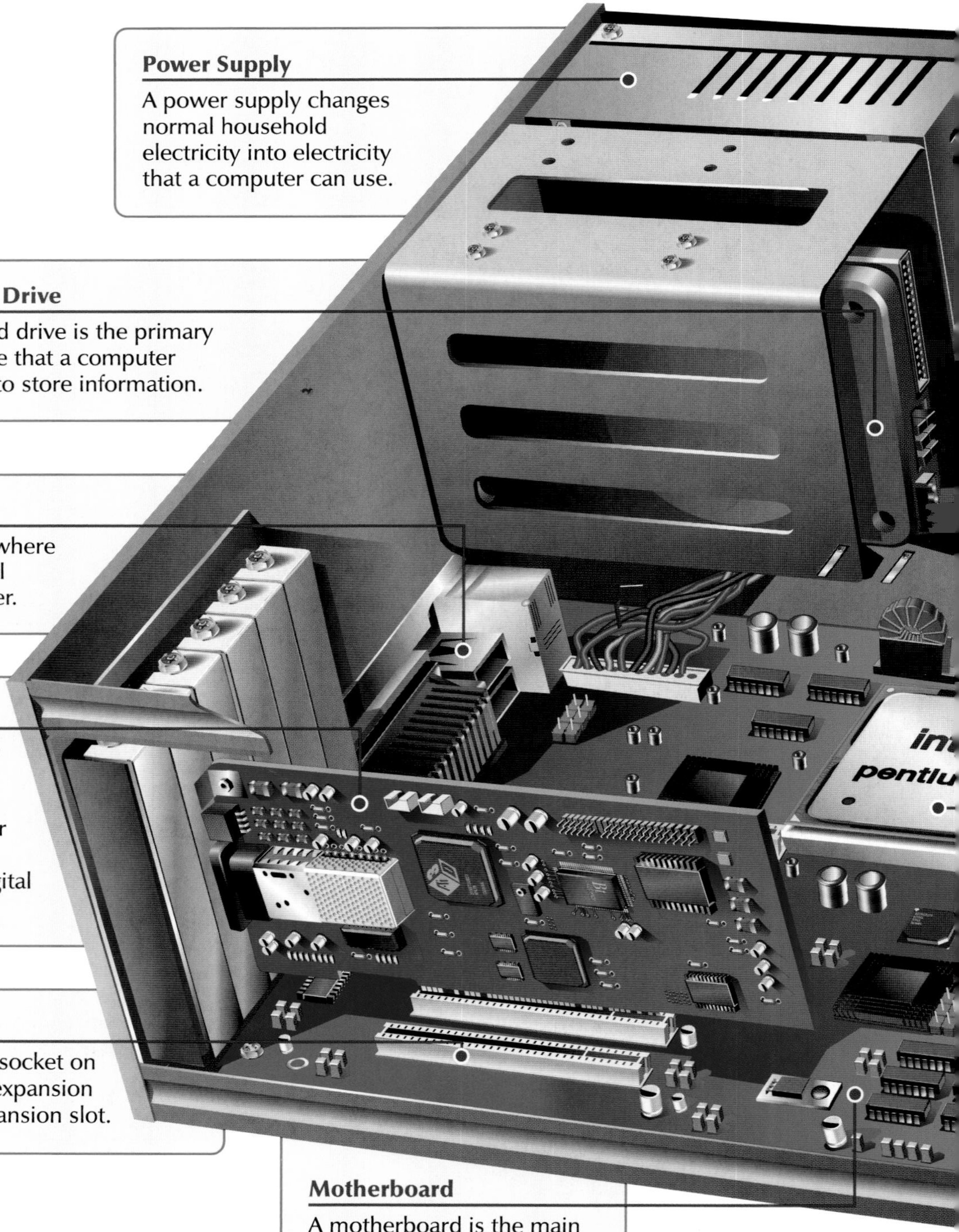

Power Supply

A power supply changes normal household electricity into electricity that a computer can use.

Hard Drive

A hard drive is the primary device that a computer uses to store information.

Port

A port is a connector where you plug in an external device such as a printer.

Expansion Card

An expansion card allows you to add new features to a computer. For example, an expansion card can add high-speed ports to your computer so you can connect high-speed devices such as a digital camcorder or an MP3 jukebox.

Expansion Slot

An expansion slot is a socket on the motherboard. An expansion card plugs into an expansion slot.

Motherboard

A motherboard is the main circuit board of a computer. All electrical components plug into the motherboard.

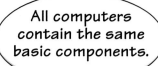

All computers contain the same basic components.

Combo Drive

A combo drive combines the functions of a CD drive and a DVD drive into one unit. A combo drive can read and store information on CDs as well as read DVDs.

CD-ROM Drive

A CD-ROM drive can read information on CDs.

Memory Card Reader

A memory card reader can read and store information on memory cards.

Floppy Drive

A floppy drive stores and retrieves information on floppy disks.

Drive Bay

A drive bay is a space inside the computer case where a hard drive, floppy drive, combo drive, CD-ROM drive and/or memory card reader sits.

Central Processing Unit (CPU)

A CPU is the main chip in a computer. The CPU processes instructions, performs calculations and manages the flow of information through a computer.

Random Access Memory (RAM)

RAM temporarily stores information inside a computer. This information is lost when you turn off the computer.

COMPUTER CASE

A computer case contains the major components of a computer.

DESKTOP CASE

A desktop case usually sits on a desk, under a monitor. Desktop cases were once very popular but are no longer widely available.

TOWER CASE

A tower case can sit on a desk next to a monitor or sit on the floor. Placing a tower case on the floor provides more desk space, but can be less convenient for inserting and removing items such as CDs and DVDs. Tower cases come in different sizes.

When choosing a case, look for a case that is well ventilated to keep the components inside cool. Also make sure the case has enough room to accommodate features you may want to add in the future.

NOTEBOOK

A notebook computer is a small, lightweight computer that is powered by a rechargeable battery, so it is easily transportable. A notebook has a built-in keyboard, pointing device, speakers and screen.

ALL-IN-ONE CASE

An all-in-one case contains all the major computer components, such as a monitor and hard drive, in a single unit.

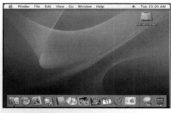

POWER SUPPLY

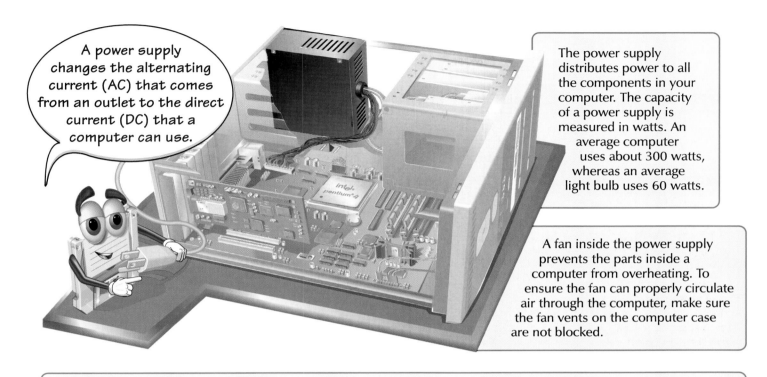

A power supply changes the alternating current (AC) that comes from an outlet to the direct current (DC) that a computer can use.

The power supply distributes power to all the components in your computer. The capacity of a power supply is measured in watts. An average computer uses about 300 watts, whereas an average light bulb uses 60 watts.

A fan inside the power supply prevents the parts inside a computer from overheating. To ensure the fan can properly circulate air through the computer, make sure the fan vents on the computer case are not blocked.

PROTECT YOUR EQUIPMENT

Changes in electrical power can damage equipment and information. Changes in electrical power include blackouts, brownouts and surges. Blackouts are a complete loss of power. Brownouts are a brief, sharp reduction in power. Surges are a brief, sharp increase in power.

Surge Protector

A surge protector, or surge suppressor, guards a computer against surges. These fluctuations happen most often during storms, peak electrical demands and your own household use.

UPS

An Uninterruptible Power Supply (UPS) protects a computer from blackouts, brownouts and surges. A UPS contains a battery that stores electrical power. If the power is interrupted, the battery can run the computer for a short time so you can save your information.

PORTS

A port is a connector at the back or front of a computer where you plug in an external device such as a printer. This allows instructions and data to flow between the computer and the device.

MOUSE PORT

A mouse port, which is also known as a PS/2 port, connects a mouse.

KEYBOARD PORT

A keyboard port, which is also known as a PS/2 port, connects a keyboard.

PARALLEL PORT

A parallel port, which is also known as a printer port or LPT port, can connect an older printer or an older scanner. On newer computers, parallel ports have been replaced with USB (Universal Serial Bus) and FireWire ports. Some newer computers do not have any parallel ports. Parallel ports are also referred to as legacy ports, which means these ports are outdated but are still in use on some computers.

SERIAL PORT

A serial port, which is also known as a COM port, can connect an older mouse or a modem. On newer computers, serial ports have been replaced with USB (Universal Serial Bus) and FireWire ports. Some newer computers do not have any serial ports. Serial ports are also referred to as legacy ports, which means these ports are outdated but are still in use on some computers.

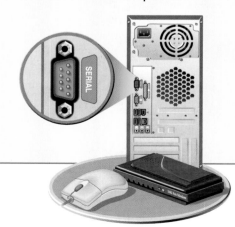

MONITOR PORT

A monitor port connects a monitor. You can connect a monitor using an analog or digital connection.

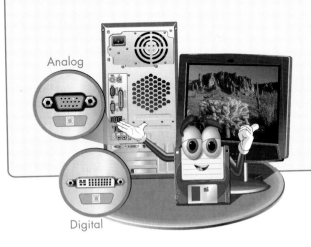

Analog

Digital

SOUND PORTS

Sound ports allow you to connect speakers, a microphone and an external sound source, such as a stereo system.

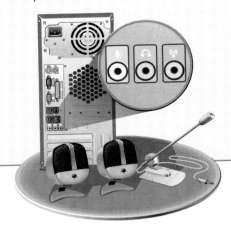

MODEM PORT

A modem port, which looks like a telephone jack, connects a modem so you can send and receive faxes from your computer and access the Internet through a telephone line. There may be a telephone jack beside the modem port where you can plug in your regular telephone.

LINE

ETHERNET (NETWORK) PORT

An Ethernet (network) port, which looks like a large telephone jack, allows you to connect the computer to a network or a high-speed Internet connection.

ETHERNET

USB PORT

A Universal Serial Bus (USB) port is a high-speed port that can connect most types of devices, including a printer, mouse, joystick and MP3 player. USB can transfer information at a speed of up to 12 megabits per second (Mbps).

USB 2.0 ports, which look the same as USB ports but are much faster, are also available. USB 2.0 can transfer information at a speed of up to 480 Mbps—40 times as fast as the original USB. USB 2.0 ports can connect USB devices as well as faster USB 2.0 devices, such as an external hard drive and an MP3 jukebox.

Most new computers come with at least two USB 2.0 ports. One or more USB 2.0 ports are located on the front of the computer to make it easy for you to connect devices.

FIREWIRE PORT

A FireWire port is a high-speed port that allows you to connect many devices that require fast data transfer speeds, including a digital camcorder, an external hard drive and an MP3 jukebox. Some electronic devices, such as DVD players and high-definition television sets, can also connect to a computer through a FireWire port.

The original version of FireWire, known as FireWire 400 or 1394, has 6 pins. FireWire 400 can transfer information at a speed of up to 400 megabits per second (Mbps) over a distance of up to 15 feet. Most new computers come with at least one FireWire 400 port.

The newer FireWire version, known as FireWire 800 or 1394b, has 9 pins. FireWire 800 can transfer information at a speed of up to 800 Mbps—twice as fast as FireWire 400—over a distance of up to 300 feet with special cabling. FireWire 800 is commonly used to connect fast external hard drives.

ADVANTAGES OF USB AND FIREWIRE PORTS

Plug and Play

USB and FireWire ports allow you to connect new devices to your computer quickly and easily. When you plug a device into a USB or FireWire port, the computer automatically detects and installs the device.

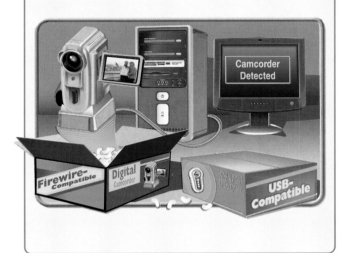

Connect Multiple Devices

Many USB and FireWire devices have built-in ports that allow you to connect additional USB or FireWire devices. Connecting one device to another in a series is known as daisy chaining devices. Daisy chaining is ideal if you do not have enough USB or FireWire ports on your computer to attach all your devices to the computer directly or if you simply want to reduce the number of wires connecting to your computer. A single USB port can support up to 127 daisy-chained devices, while a single FireWire port can support up to 63 daisy-chained devices.

ADD PORTS TO YOUR COMPUTER

If you have a device that cannot connect to your computer because your computer does not have the appropriate port, you can often add an expansion card, which is a circuit board containing the port you need, to your computer. You may also be able to purchase an adapter for the device, which plugs into an existing port on your computer.

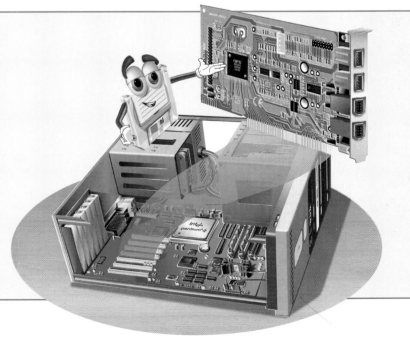

EXPANSION CARD

An expansion card is a circuit board that allows you to add new features to a computer.

An expansion card is also called an expansion board.

EXPANSION SLOT

An expansion slot is a socket where you plug in an expansion card.

The number of expansion slots your computer has affects the number of cards you can add to the computer. Before you buy a computer, make sure it has enough empty expansion slots for your future needs.

CONNECT DEVICES

Most expansion cards are accessible from the back or front of a computer and contain ports where you can plug in devices. For example, you can transfer video to your computer by connecting your digital camcorder to a port on the FireWire card.

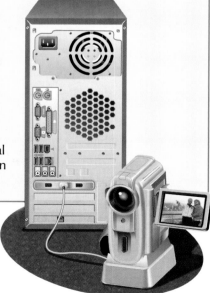

You can add expansion cards to increase the capabilities of your computer.

COMMONLY ADDED EXPANSION CARDS

High-End Video

High-end video cards produce faster and better quality images and video than the standard video card included with most computers. A high-end video card is useful when playing graphic-intensive games or using photo or video editing software.

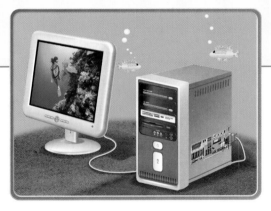

FireWire or USB 2.0

FireWire and USB (Universal Serial Bus) 2.0 cards allow a computer to easily connect to devices that require fast data transfer speeds, including a digital camcorder, MP3 jukebox and external hard drive. You can buy cards that include both FireWire and USB 2.0 on one card. FireWire is also referred to as 1394.

High-End Sound

A high-end sound card produces better quality sound than the standard sound card included with most computers. A high-end sound card includes surround sound capabilities and allows you to connect multiple speakers to your computer.

Network Interface

A network interface card allows you to connect computers to share information and equipment on a network. A network interface card also allows a computer to connect to the Internet through a high-speed connection.

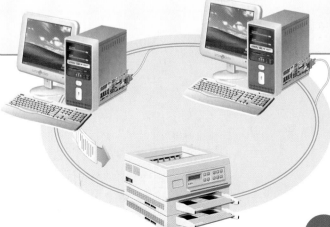

PURCHASE A NEW COMPUTER

There are many factors to consider when purchasing a new computer.

When buying a new computer, you should find out if the seller will help you if you experience problems with the computer after you purchase it.

CONSIDERATIONS

Intended Use

Before you choose a computer, you must first determine what you want to be able to do with the computer. For example, if you plan to do a lot of traveling, consider purchasing a notebook computer. If you plan to play a lot of games, consider buying a computer with a good-quality video card for displaying graphics.

Cost

The cost of a computer depends on your needs. You can purchase a standard home computer for under $500. If you want a faster computer with more features, you will need to spend more money.

The price of a computer usually includes a keyboard, mouse and speakers, but often does not include a monitor.

Retail Stores versus Online Computer Stores

Retail stores include Best Buy, CompUSA and some specialty retailers. Retail stores allow you to compare different computer models in person and take your new computer home the same day.

Online stores include Dell (www.dell.com), Hewlett-Packard (www.hp.com) and Gateway (www.gateway.com). Online stores allow you to customize a computer to suit your needs, but can take a week or more to ship the computer to you.

UPGRADE A COMPUTER

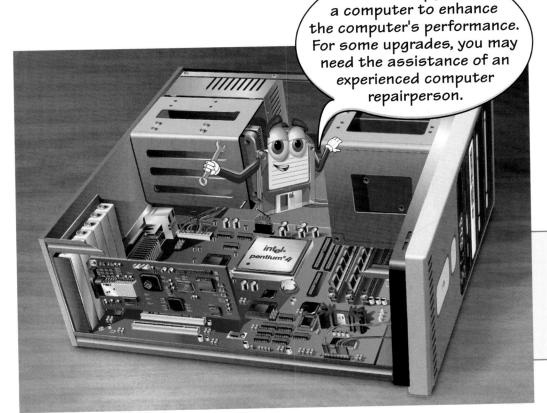

You can upgrade a computer to enhance the computer's performance. For some upgrades, you may need the assistance of an experienced computer repairperson.

Upgrading usually refers to adding a new component, such as a recordable DVD drive, FireWire card or high-end video card, to increase the capabilities of the computer.

CONSIDERATIONS

Cost

You should always determine the cost of an upgrade before performing the upgrade. If you are planning a major upgrade, such as replacing the CPU or hard drive, you may want to consider purchasing a new computer.

Effective Upgrade

Increasing the amount of memory in a computer is the most effective upgrade you can perform. Doubling the existing memory in a computer can significantly increase the performance of the computer.

CHAPTER 2

INPUT AND OUTPUT DEVICES

What type of printer is best for you? What is a Bluetooth wireless device and why would you want one? This chapter will answer these questions and more.

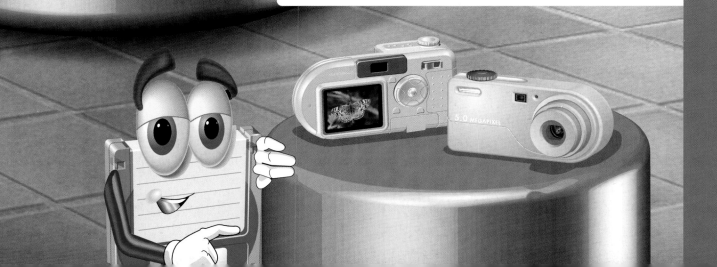

A mouse is a handheld device that allows you to select and move items on your screen.

You can buy a mouse in various shapes, colors and sizes. When you move a mouse on your desk, the pointer (⬚) on the screen moves in the same direction.

MOUSE FEATURES

Buttons

Most mice have two buttons that you can press and release, or "click," to perform an action. Some mice have more than two buttons. These additional buttons may be pre-programmed or you may be able to program the buttons to perform specific tasks, such as starting a Web browser.

Wheels

Most mice have a wheel between the left and right buttons. You can use this wheel to scroll through information in documents and on the Web.

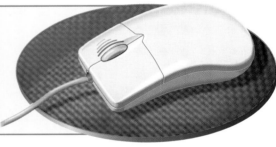

Connection Types

A mouse can connect to a computer through a serial, PS/2 (mouse) or USB (Universal Serial Bus) connection. Some mice run on a battery and connect wirelessly to the computer. When you move a wireless mouse, the mouse sends signals to your computer or to a device attached to your computer. A wireless mouse reduces the clutter on your desk by eliminating the mouse cord and allows you to sit farther away from your computer.

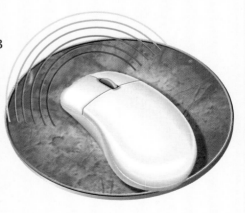

TYPES OF MICE

Mechanical Mouse

A mechanical mouse detects mouse movement using a ball on the bottom of the mouse which rolls as the mouse is moved. This type of mouse needs regular cleaning to remove dust and dirt from inside the mouse and ensure smooth motion. You should use a mouse pad to provide a smooth surface for moving the mouse and to reduce the amount of dirt that enters the mouse.

Optical Mouse

An optical mouse detects mouse movement using a beam of light. This type of mouse does not contain any moving parts that can wear out or require cleaning. You do not need to use a mouse pad when using an optical mouse, but for best results you should use the mouse on a flat surface that is a solid color.

OTHER POINTING DEVICES

Trackball

A trackball is an upside-down mouse that remains stationary on your desk. You roll the ball with your fingers or palm to move the pointer on the screen. Trackballs usually include buttons that you can use the same way you use the buttons on a mouse. A trackball is a great alternative to a mouse when you have limited desk space.

Tablet

A tablet consists of a flat surface and a pen, called a stylus. When you move the stylus on the surface of the tablet, the mouse pointer moves on the computer screen. Tablets are most often used for performing tasks that require speed and precision, such as graphic design and image editing. Tablets, also known as digitizer tablets and graphics tablets, also often come with a mouse that you can use in addition to the stylus.

KEYBOARD

The keys on a keyboard allow you to enter information and instructions into a computer.

KEYBOARD FEATURES

Connection Types

A keyboard can connect to a computer through a PS/2 (keyboard) or USB (Universal Serial Bus) connection. Some keyboards run on a battery and connect wirelessly to the computer. A wireless keyboard reduces clutter on your desk by eliminating the keyboard cord and allows you to sit up to 30 feet away from a computer.

QWERTY Keyboards

The most common type of keyboard is known as a QWERTY keyboard, which refers to how the keys are positioned on the keyboard. On this type of keyboard, the first six characters on the top line of alphabetic keys are Q, W, E, R, T and Y.

Finger Position Guides

Most keyboards have small bumps on the F and J keys that help you position your fingers without looking at the keyboard.

PREVENT TYPING INJURIES

Ergonomic Keyboards

Ergonomic keyboards, which consist of separate sections of keys, allow you to position your hands more naturally so you can work more comfortably. Ergonomic keyboards can also help prevent a repetitive strain injury, such as carpal tunnel syndrome.

Wrist Rests

You can use a wrist rest with your keyboard to ensure your wrists remain elevated and straight while you type. Using a wrist rest with a keyboard will prevent you from resting your wrists on the edge of a desk—a position which can cause wrist injury. Some keyboards come with a built-in wrist rest. You can also purchase a wrist rest for your keyboard separately.

Take Breaks

You should take frequent breaks when typing to prevent hand and wrist strain that can lead to typing injuries. You should stretch or perform other tasks for 15 minutes after every hour or two of typing.

CLEAN A KEYBOARD

Over time, dust and dirt can accumulate on your keyboard, causing the keys to stick or not respond when pressed. To remove dust and dirt, you can run a vacuum cleaner over the keys.

The plastic outer surface of the keyboard can be cleaned with a damp cloth. You should not attempt to open your keyboard to clean the inside, as this can damage the keyboard.

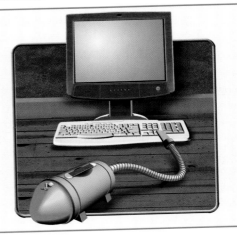

Most keyboards have 101 keys and include some or all of the following keys.

Function Keys

These keys allow you to quickly perform specific tasks. For example, in many programs, you can press F1 to display help information.

Hot Keys

Each of these buttons allows you to perform a specific task, such as opening your Web browser, launching your e-mail program or adjusting your computer's volume setting.

MAIL   INTERNET   MUSIC   PICTURE
S1   S2   S3   S4

Escape Key

You can press Esc to quit a task you are performing.

Tab Key

You can press Tab to move to the next tabbed location in a document.

Caps Lock and Shift Keys

These keys allow you to enter text in uppercase (ABC) and lowercase (abc) letters.

Press Caps Lock to change the case of all letters you type. Press the key again to return to the original case.

Press Shift in combination with another key to type an uppercase letter.

Ctrl and Alt Keys

You can use the Ctrl or Alt key in combination with another key to perform a specific task. For example, in some programs, you can press Ctrl and S to save a document.

Windows Key (⊞)

You can press this key to quickly display the Start menu when using the Windows operating system, such as Windows XP.

Spacebar

You can press the Spacebar to insert a blank space.

Backspace Key

You can press `Backspace` to remove the character to the left of the cursor.

Insert Key

You can press `Insert` to type over existing text in a document. Press the key again to stop your typing from replacing existing text.

Delete Key

You can press `Delete` to remove the character to the right of the cursor or delete the selected item.

Status Lights

These lights indicate whether the `Num Lock` and `Caps Lock` features are on or off.

Application Key ( )

You can press this key to quickly display the shortcut menu for an item on your screen.

Enter Key

You can press `Enter` to tell the computer to carry out a task. In a word processing program, press this key to start a new line or paragraph.

Arrow Keys

These keys allow you to move the cursor around the screen.

Numeric Keypad

When the `Num Lock` light is on, you can use the number keys (`0` through `9`) to enter numbers. When the `Num Lock` light is off, you can use these keys to move the cursor around the screen. To turn the light on or off, press `Num Lock`.

PRINTER

A printer is a device that produces a paper copy of the information displayed on a computer screen.

You can use a printer to produce letters, invoices, newsletters, photos, transparencies, labels, envelopes and more.

ALL-IN-ONE PRINTERS

Features

An all-in-one printer can perform more than one task. Most all-in-one printers can work as a printer, scanner and photocopier, while some can also work as a fax machine. All-in-one printers are less expensive and require much less space than the multiple pieces of equipment that perform the same tasks. Although all-in-one printers can perform many tasks, they may not offer all the features provided by a standalone printer, scanner, photocopier and fax machine. All-in-one printers are also known as multifunction printers.

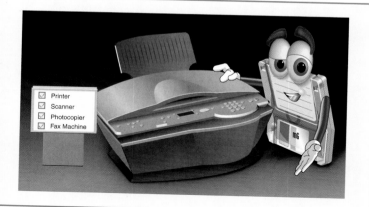

- ☑ Printer
- ☑ Scanner
- ☑ Photocopier
- ☑ Fax Machine

All-In-One Printer Considerations

• Many all-in-one printers allow you to make black-and-white photocopies as well as color photocopies.

• You can buy all-in-one printers in inkjet or laser printer format.

• Some all-in-one printers include a sheetfed scanner, which scans single sheets of paper. Other all-in-one printers include a flatbed scanner, which allows you to place thick items you want to scan on a flat surface.

• If you want to use an all-in-one printer as a standalone fax machine, look for a complete set of fax controls on the printer so you can send and receive faxes when your computer is turned off.

INKJET PRINTERS

How They Work

An inkjet printer sprays ink onto a page and prints each page one line at a time. An inkjet printer produces good-quality text and graphics and high-quality photos.

Cost and Speed

An inkjet printer is less expensive to buy than a laser printer, but the cost per page is more expensive. An inkjet printer is also slower than a laser printer, especially when printing long documents.

Ink

Inkjet printers use ink stored in cartridges. Color inkjet printers use four separate colors, which include cyan, magenta, yellow and black, to produce printed pages. Some inkjet printers use two ink cartridges—one containing only black ink and one containing all the other colors—while other inkjet printers use a separate ink cartridge for each color. Using a separate ink cartridge for each color can save you money since you do not have to throw out all the colors when one color runs out.

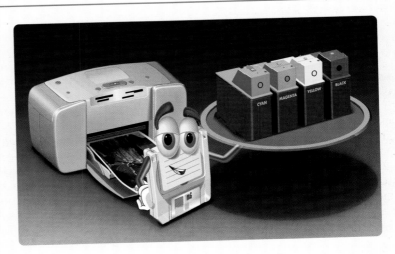

Purchase an Ink Cartridge

When an ink cartridge runs out, you need to buy a new ink cartridge designed for your printer. You can save money and the environment by having an ink cartridge refilled with ink instead of buying a new cartridge.

Ink cartridges have an expiry date. Before you buy a new ink cartridge, make sure the cartridge has not expired.

LASER PRINTERS

How They Work

A laser printer uses a laser beam to print an entire page all at once. This allows laser printers to offer fast print speeds, which makes them ideal for printing long, complex documents.

Quality & Cost

Laser printers produce high-quality text and graphics and good-quality photos. You can buy color and monochrome, or black-and-white, laser printers. A laser printer is more expensive to buy than an inkjet printer, but the cost per page is less expensive.

LED Printers

LED (Light-Emitting Diode) printers are similar to laser printers but they do not use a laser beam. LED printers are generally less expensive and smaller than laser printers.

Toner

Laser printers use a fine powdered ink, called toner, which comes in a cartridge. Black-and-white laser printers use one cartridge that stores black ink. Color laser printers usually have a separate cartridge for each color—cyan, magenta, yellow and black. When a toner cartridge runs out, you will need to buy a new cartridge designed for your printer. You can save money and the environment by having a cartridge refilled with toner instead of buying a new cartridge.

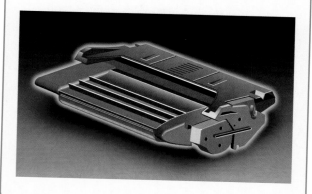

Printer Languages

A printer language describes how text and graphics should appear on a printed page. There are two types of laser printer languages—PCL and PostScript.

PCL

Most laser printers come with Printer Control Language (PCL). A page printed on a PCL printer may look different when printed on another laser printer.

PostScript

Some laser printers offer the PostScript printer language. A page will print exactly the same way on any PostScript printer.

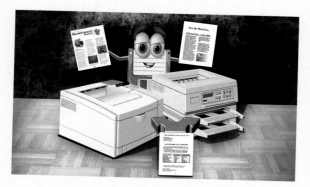

PHOTO PRINTERS

Print Photos

A photo printer is usually an inkjet printer that is specifically designed to print photographs. Photo printers can produce true photo quality, which means photos printed on a photo printer are indistinguishable from prints produced at photo shops.

Capabilities

Photo printers have a wide range of capabilities. For example, some printers allow you to add borders to your printed photos.

Ink

Photo printers use the same ink cartridges as inkjet printers. Photo printers use the standard colors—cyan, magenta, yellow and black—but many also offer additional colors such as light magenta and light cyan. More ink colors help to widen the range of colors the printer can produce and make colors such as skin tones easier to reproduce. If you plan to print a lot of black-and-white photos, look for a printer that uses a gray ink.

Print Without a Computer

Some photo printers allow you to connect a digital camera directly to the printer. You can also find photo printers that come with memory card slots that allow you to insert a memory card from a digital camera, eliminating the need for a computer to print photos. Photo printers can include small screens with menus that allow you to preview and crop your pictures, choose which pictures you want to print, reduce red-eye and more.

CHOOSE A PRINTER

Speed

The speed of a printer indicates how quickly a printer can print pages and is measured in pages per minute (ppm). Printer manufacturers usually indicate the speed at which a printer can produce black-and-white documents. If a printer can print in color, the speed for color documents is also usually given. If a printer can print photos, a manufacturer may indicate the print speed for a 4 x 6 photo and an 8 x 10 photo in seconds or minutes.

Resolution

The resolution of a printer determines the quality of the text and images a printer can produce. A higher resolution results in sharper, more detailed images. The resolution of a printer is measured in dots per inch (dpi) and is usually expressed by two numbers, such as 1200 x 600 dpi, or by only one number, such as 600 dpi.

Text Documents & Photos
600 dpi

Artwork
1200 dpi

Black & White versus Color

If a printer can print in color, the manufacturer will usually provide the resolution for printing black-and-white documents as well as color documents. Generally, a resolution of 600 dpi is sufficient for most text documents and photos and 1200 dpi works well for printing artwork.

Sheet Capacity

Printers can hold a certain amount of paper at one time. A lower sheet capacity means you will have to refill the paper tray more often.

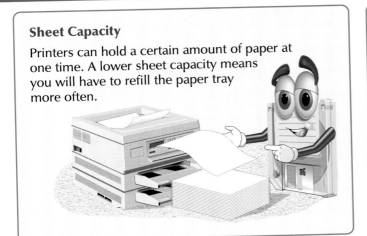

Paper Size

Most printers can print on 8.5 x 11 inch paper. Some printers can print on larger paper sizes, such as legal paper, which is 8.5 x 14 inches. Make sure the printer you choose can print the size of paper you plan to use.

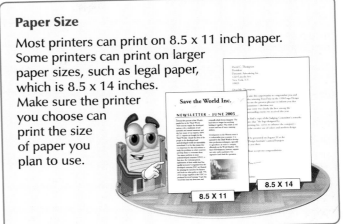

Memory

Laser printers and some inkjet printers store documents you select to print in built-in memory before printing. The amount of memory a printer offers is usually measured in megabytes (MB). More memory increases the printing speed when printing long or complex documents. Some printers allow you to add memory modules to the printer. Printer manufacturers usually indicate the amount of memory installed and the maximum amount of memory you can add to a printer.

Types of Paper

Each printer can print on different types of paper and materials, such as envelopes, labels, photo paper, transparencies and iron-on transfers. Make sure the printer you choose can print on the type of paper and materials you plan to use.

Types of Connections

Printers usually connect to a computer through a Universal Serial Bus (USB), parallel or network (Ethernet) connection. A parallel port offers the slowest type of connection to a computer. A network connection is useful if you want to connect a printer directly to a network so more than one computer can use the printer.

MONITOR

A monitor displays text and images generated by a computer.

The viewing area of a monitor is also known as the screen.

TYPES OF MONITORS

CRT Monitors

Cathode Ray Tube (CRT) monitors use the same technology as most television sets. CRT monitors are relatively inexpensive and display brighter images than LCD monitors, but are heavy, difficult to move and take up a lot of desk space. CRT monitors also use more electricity and emit more electromagnetic radiation than LCD monitors. CRT monitors are becoming less popular as the price of LCD monitors decreases.

LCD Monitors

Liquid Crystal Display (LCD) monitors use the same type of display found in notebook computers. These monitors use active matrix technology, or thin film transistor (TFT) technology, to produce images. LCD monitors, also known as flat panel monitors, are thin, stylish and lightweight. They also take up less desk space, use less electricity and emit less electromagnetic radiation than CRT monitors. LCD monitors, however, are relatively expensive and can be difficult to view from the side and in bright sunlight.

SIZE

Common Sizes

The size of a monitor is measured diagonally across the screen. Monitor sizes range from 15 to 30 inches, but are typically 17 or 19 inches. Larger monitors are more expensive, but can display more information at once.

Manufacturers often advertise the diagonal measurement of the picture tube inside a CRT monitor, which is one to two inches larger than the viewing area. Make sure you are aware of the size of the viewing area before purchasing a CRT monitor. LCD monitors always indicate the size of the viewing area.

RESOLUTION

Commonly Used Resolutions

The resolution is the number of horizontal and vertical dots, called pixels, displayed on a screen. The most commonly used resolutions are 1,024 x 768, which is also known as XGA (Extended Graphics Array), and 1,280 x 1,024, which is also known as SXGA (Super XGA).

Manufacturers indicate the native resolution of an LCD monitor, which indicates the resolution that will provide the best display.

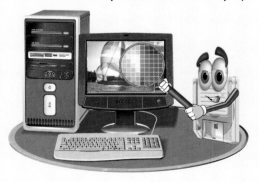

Adjust the Resolution

Most CRT monitors allow you to adjust the resolution to suit your needs. The resolution you choose depends on the size of your monitor and the amount of information you want to display on your screen at once. Lower resolutions display larger images so you can see information more clearly, while higher resolutions display smaller images so you can display more information on your screen at once. You will usually not change the resolution of an LCD monitor since this can greatly reduce the image quality.

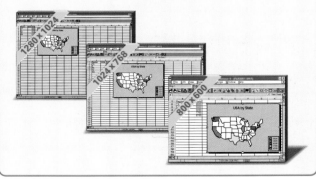

Dot Pitch

The dot pitch is the distance between dots, called pixels, that make up an image on a screen. The dot pitch determines the sharpness of images on a monitor and is measured in millimeters (mm). The smaller the dot pitch, the sharper the images. For example, a CRT monitor with a dot pitch of 0.26 mm or less is ideal.

Brightness

The brightness of a monitor is measured in candelas per square meter (cd/m^2) or nits. A higher number indicates a brighter screen. Brighter monitors display richer colors, function better in locations with a lot of natural light and help reduce eyestrain. For example, a brightness of over 250 cd/m^2 is ideal for an LCD monitor.

Contrast Ratio

For an LCD monitor, the contrast ratio refers to the difference between the brightest white and the darkest black that a monitor can produce. The higher the contrast ratio, the better the monitor's ability to show subtle color details, which is ideal for playing games and watching movies. An LCD monitor with a contrast ratio of at least 400:1 is ideal.

Controls

A monitor has controls you can use to adjust the images displayed on the screen. For example, you can use the controls on a CRT monitor to change the brightness and contrast of the display. The controls are usually located on the bottom edge of the front of a CRT monitor, but can also be accessed through an on-screen menu.

Tilt and Swivel Base

Many monitors allow you to tilt the monitor up and down and swivel the monitor from side to side to obtain a better viewing angle and help reduce the glare from overhead lighting.

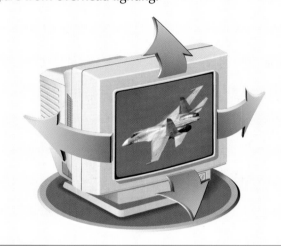

Monitor Rotation

You can physically rotate some LCD monitors from landscape mode, in which the monitor is wider than it is tall, to portrait mode, in which the monitor is taller than it is wide. This feature can be useful when working with documents or browsing the Web.

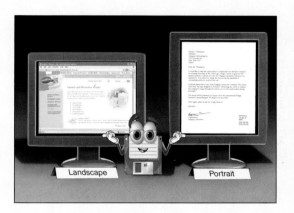

Refresh Rate

For CRT monitors, the refresh rate determines the speed that a monitor redraws, or updates, images on the screen. A higher refresh rate reduces flicker on the screen, which helps to reduce eyestrain. The refresh rate is measured in hertz (Hz) and tells you the number of times per second the monitor redraws the entire screen. A CRT monitor with a refresh rate of 72 Hz or more is recommended.

Response Time

For an LCD monitor, the response time indicates how fast the monitor can display changes on the screen. When information changes on the screen, a ghosting effect may occur, which means the previous information remains on the screen after the new information appears. The lower the response time, the faster the images on the screen update, which reduces the ghosting effect. You should look for an LCD monitor with a response time of 16 milliseconds (ms) or less.

CHOOSE A MONITOR (Continued)

Energy Star

In general, an LCD monitor uses less electricity than a CRT monitor. To help conserve even more electricity, the Environmental Protection Agency (EPA) developed an energy-saving guideline called Energy Star®. Most new CRT and LCD monitors are Energy Star compliant.

When you do not use an Energy Star monitor for a period of time, the monitor enters an energy-saving sleep mode, which uses significantly less electricity. You can awaken the monitor at any time by moving the mouse or pressing a key on the keyboard. Energy Star monitors last longer and save you money.

Monitor Filters

You can obtain a filter that fits over the front of a monitor to decrease the amount of light reflected off the computer screen and reduce eyestrain. Many filters can also block the electromagnetic radiation produced by a monitor.

Privacy filters are also available that make the screen difficult to read when viewed from an angle, which helps keep your work private.

Electromagnetic Radiation

Any device that uses electricity produces Electromagnetic Radiation (EMR). You can minimize the risk of EMR by buying a monitor that meets MPR or TCO guidelines, which define acceptable levels of EMR.

You can further minimize the risk of EMR by purchasing a smaller monitor, sitting a safe distance away from a monitor, buying an LCD monitor instead of a CRT monitor and turning off a monitor when it is not in use.

Flat-Screen

Some CRT monitors have a flat screen instead of the curved screen offered by most CRT monitors. Flat-screen CRT monitors provide a sharper image and reduce glare, but are more expensive than monitors with a curved screen.

Built-In Speakers

Some monitors have built-in speakers, which can save desk space. Keep in mind, though, that the sound quality produced by built-in speakers tends to be lower than the sound quality produced by standalone speakers.

Widescreen

Some LCD monitors have a wide screen. A wide screen is ideal for viewing widescreen DVD movies, watching high-definition television and playing games designed for widescreen play.

Digital Input

Many LCD monitors offer a digital connection, known as DVI (Digital Video Interface), between the video card and the monitor. If your computer has a digital video card, using the DVI connector to connect your LCD monitor to the computer can result in sharper images and better color quality.

If your computer does not offer a DVI connection, an LCD monitor must use an analog connection to connect to the computer. When using an analog connection, the monitor must translate the analog signal coming from the video card to a digital signal the monitor can use to display an image on the screen.

VIDEO CARD

A video card is an expansion card that generates the images displayed on a computer's monitor.

You can see the edge of a video card at the back of a computer. A video card has several ports where you can plug in external devices. The edge of your video card may look different from the video card shown here.

S-Video Port

Digital Input Port

VGA Port

A video card is also known as a graphics card, video adapter or graphics adapter.

S-Video or TV-Out Port
Allows you to connect a television or projector.

Digital Input (DVI) Port
Allows you to connect an LCD monitor or digital television.

VGA Port
Allows you to connect a CRT monitor.

VIDEO SLOTS

There are two main ways that a video card connects to a computer—by plugging into an AGP slot or into a PCIe slot.

AGP

An Accelerated Graphics Port (AGP) video card plugs into an AGP slot in a computer. The AGP slot allows the video card to communicate directly with the computer's main memory and quickly display complex images on your monitor. Currently the fastest version of AGP is AGP 8x.

PCIe

A Peripheral Component Interconnect Express (PCIe) video card plugs into a PCIe slot in a computer. PCIe allows the video card to send and receive information from the computer's main memory at the same time for fast display of images. PCIe is a newer, faster type of slot found in high-end computers. There are several versions of PCIe, but PCIe x16 is the version most often used for video cards.

INTEGRATED GRAPHICS

Many entry-level computers include integrated graphics instead of a video card. When a computer has integrated graphics, the computer's memory (RAM) is shared between processing information and displaying images. This type of graphics system reduces the overall cost of a computer but can slow down the computer's

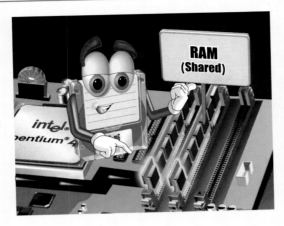

performance because the RAM is used to temporarily store video information. Integrated graphics is adequate for performing day-to-day tasks on a computer, but will not provide good performance for games or graphics-intensive applications.

HIGH-END VIDEO CARD

A high-end video card is designed to produce faster and smoother graphics when playing games or using photo or video editing software. A high-end video card has its own memory as well as a specialized chip, called a Graphics Processing Unit (GPU) or Video Processing Unit (VPU), that is optimized to produce 3D images.

A GPU allows a video card to display images on the screen without using your computer's processor, which improves your computer's overall performance. ATI and nVidia are popular high-end video card manufacturers.

TV TUNER CARD

A TV tuner card allows you to watch television programs on your computer. Most TV tuner cards also allow you to save still images and full-motion video clips from a television program on your hard drive.

A TV tuner card can be a separate expansion card that plugs into an expansion slot. Video cards that have TV tuner card capabilities built-in, known as all-in-one cards, are also available.

VIDEO CARD CONSIDERATIONS

AMOUNT OF MEMORY

A video card contains memory chips that temporarily store information before sending it to the monitor. If you use professional graphics applications or play graphics-intensive games, you should have a video card with at least 128 MB of memory.

A video card with a large amount of memory will be capable of providing a higher refresh rate, resolution and color depth than a video card with a smaller amount of memory.

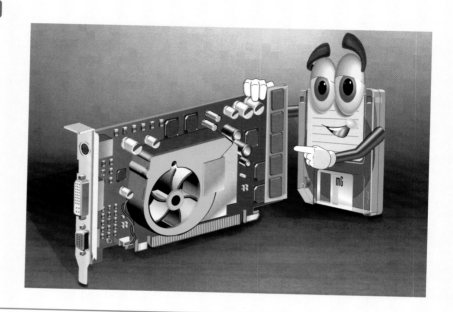

TYPE OF MEMORY

SDRAM (Synchronous Dynamic Random-Access Memory) and DDR SDRAM (Double-Data-Rate SDRAM) are the most common types of memory found on video cards. DDR SDRAM, also known as DDR, can process information approximately twice as fast as SDRAM. There are several versions of DDR used on video cards, including DDR2, DDR3 and GDDR3 (Graphics DDR3). The higher the number, the faster the memory chips can process information.

DIRECTX SUPPORT

DirectX is a set of applications that provide exceptional performance in games and videos for computers using the Windows operating system. Most video cards are optimized to support DirectX.

REFRESH RATE

The refresh rate determines the speed that a CRT monitor updates images on the screen. Your video card must be able to use the same refresh rate as your monitor. Most monitors can detect which refresh rate the video card is using and then automatically switch to the appropriate setting. A refresh rate of 72 hertz (Hz) or more is recommended.

RESOLUTION

Resolution is the number of horizontal and vertical dots, called pixels, displayed on a screen. Higher resolutions display smaller images so you can display more information on your screen at once, while lower resolutions display larger images so you can see information more clearly. Your video card must be able to use the same resolution as your monitor.

COLOR DEPTH

The video card you use determines the number of colors a monitor can display. More colors result in more realistic images. Most video cards sold today are capable of supporting 32-bit color, or over 4 billion colors.

If your video card does not have adequate memory, you may not be able to use a high color depth if your computer is set at a high resolution.

MODEM

A modem allows a computer to send and receive information through a telephone line.

A modem translates computer information into a form that can transmit over telephone lines. A modem also translates the information it receives into a form a computer can understand.

TYPES OF MODEMS

Internal Modem

Most new computers come with an internal modem. An internal modem may be a circuit board that plugs into an expansion slot inside a computer or may be built into the motherboard of a computer. An internal modem is generally less expensive than an external modem.

External Modem

An external modem is a small device that connects to a computer by a USB (Universal Serial Bus) or serial connection. Modems that use a USB connection are easier to set up than modems that use a serial connection. An external modem takes up room on your desk, but can be moved and used with other computers. Most external modems have lights to indicate the status of the modem and whether the modem is working properly.

SPEEDS AND STANDARDS

Most modems available today can transfer information at speeds up to 56 Kilobits per second (56K), depending on the quality of the telephone line connection.

Modem standards ensure that modems made by different manufacturers can communicate with each other. V.92 is the current standard for 56K modems.

MODEM FEATURES

Phone Line Use

You can use the same telephone line for telephone and modem calls. If you have a call waiting feature, you can use software, often referred to as modem-on-hold software, that allows you to accept an incoming telephone call without losing your modem connection. If you do not use this type of software, make sure the call waiting feature is disabled when you use the modem, since the call waiting feature could disrupt the modem connection.

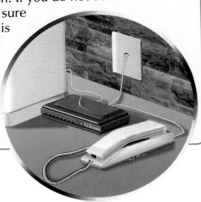

Access Information

You can use a modem to connect to the Internet to browse the Web and exchange e-mail. When traveling or at home, you can use a modem to access information, such as office files and e-mail, stored on the network at work.

Send and Receive Faxes

Most modems can send and receive faxes. With a fax modem, you can create a document on your computer and then fax the document to another computer or fax machine. When you receive a fax using a modem, you can view the fax on your computer screen, which helps to conserve paper.

Voice Capabilities

Some modems allow you to connect your telephone to the modem so you can use a computer to send and receive telephone calls. You can attach a microphone to your computer to use the computer as a hands-free telephone or use special software to turn your computer into an answering machine.

SOUND CARD

A sound card allows a computer to play, record and process sounds.

Most computers come with basic sound capabilities, which are often built into the main circuit board of a computer. You can add a higher quality sound card to a computer to greatly improve the sound generated by the computer.

A sound card is also called a sound board or audio card.

SOUND CARD APPLICATIONS

Play Sounds

A sound card allows you to hear music when using your computer to play music CDs. A sound card also allows you to hear speech, sound effects and music when playing games and when viewing videos, DVD movies, Web pages and multimedia presentations. Sound cards also allow you to hear sounds generated by a computer, such as the "You've Got Mail" recording when you receive an e-mail message.

Record Sounds

Sound cards allow you to record music from music CDs as well as use a microphone to record your own voice or sound effects. You can add the sounds you record to documents, presentations and home movies you create.

Process Sounds

Sound cards allow you to connect a musical instrument, such as an electronic keyboard, to a computer to use the computer to compose music. You can also use a sound card and voice recognition software to be able to use your voice to instruct a computer to perform tasks. Sound cards also allow you to talk to friends, family members and colleagues over the Internet.

SOUND CARD CONNECTIONS

A sound card has several connections, called jacks or ports, where you can plug in external devices. Here are some common connections you will see on a sound card.

Microphone In

This jack allows you to connect a microphone to record speech and other sounds.

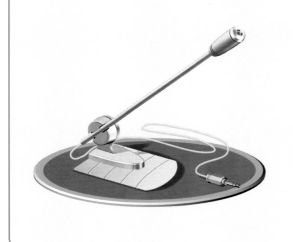

Line In or Digital In

The line in jack allows you to connect an external sound source, such as a VCR or tape deck. A digital in jack allows you to connect an external digital sound source, such as a CD-ROM player or game console, which provides superior sound quality.

FireWire and USB

Some sound cards offer one or more FireWire or USB (Universal Serial Bus) ports that allow you to connect devices such as a digital camera or digital camcorder. A sound card that includes a FireWire or USB port provides your computer with an extra port and is especially useful if your computer does not already have the port.

Line Out or Digital Out

The line out jack allows you to connect speakers, headphones or an external receiver, or amplifier, which can connect to speakers or a home stereo system. A digital out jack allows you to connect an external digital sound source, which provides superior sound quality.

SOUND CARD

TYPES OF SOUND CARDS

Internal Sound Card

You can enhance the quality of sound generated by a computer by adding a higher quality, internal sound card. An internal sound card is a circuit board that plugs into an expansion slot inside a computer. Most internal sounds cards are PCI (Peripheral Component Interconnect) sound cards, which defines the type of slot the sound card plugs into.

External Sound Device

An external sound device usually connects to a computer through a USB (Universal Serial Bus) connection. An external sound device takes up room on your desk, but is easier to set up and can be moved and used with other computers. External sound devices usually produce higher quality sound than internal sound cards, but are generally more expensive.

SURROUND SOUND

Basic sound cards allow you to connect two speakers to produce stereo sound. Many sound cards now offer surround sound, which allows you to place multiple speakers around the computer so the sound generated by the computer "surrounds" you. Surround sound is ideal when watching movies and playing games. Two popular types of surround sound include Dolby Digital and DTS.

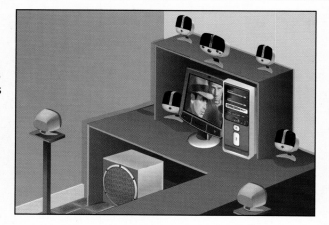

5.1, 6.1 and 7.1

5.1 surround sound allows you to connect five speakers as well as a subwoofer to produce the low sounds. The .1 refers to the subwoofer. You can also obtain sound cards that provide 6.1 and 7.1 surround sound, allowing you to connect six or seven speakers and a subwoofer to the sound card.

SOUND QUALITY

Signal-To-Noise Ratio (SNR)

The Signal-to-Noise Ratio (SNR) compares the sound played, known as the signal, to the unwanted noise you hear when no sound is played, such as humming, hissing and crackling noises. The signal-to-noise ratio is measured in decibels (dB). A higher signal-to-noise ratio means more signal and less noise, resulting in better sound quality. A high-end sound card will have a signal-to-noise ratio of 100 dB or more.

Number Of Bits

The number of bits indicates the number of sounds a sound card can process. The higher the number of bits, the higher the quality of the sound. For example, 16-bit refers to 65,536 sound levels and 24-bit refers to 16.7 million sound levels. Most high-end sound cards are 24-bit.

Sampling Rate

The sampling rate of a sound card indicates how often samples are taken from the original sound to digitally recreate the sound. The sampling rate is measured in kilohertz (kHz). Higher sampling rates result in more realistic sound. High-end sound cards offer a sampling rate of 192 kHz.

SOUND BLASTER

Sound Blaster sound cards are the industry standard for sound cards. Most sound cards and software applications are marked as Sound Blaster compatible. Make sure the sound card you buy is Sound Blaster compatible.

API SUPPORT

Application Programming Interfaces (APIs) are special functions a game or program will use to communicate with your sound card. If your game or program uses specific APIs, your sound card must support them. Some popular APIs include DirectSound, EAX and MacroFX.

GAMING DEVICES

Gaming devices allow you to control movement and actions in computer games. Gaming devices are also known as game controllers.

Each type of gaming device is best suited for certain types of games. The types of games you plan on playing can help you decide which type of gaming device you should consider buying.

TYPES OF CONNECTIONS

Most gaming devices connect to a computer through a USB (Universal Serial Bus) connection, which allows you to plug in the device and have the computer instantly set up the device for you.

You can also buy wireless gaming devices that allow you greater freedom of movement when playing games because the device's cord does not get in your way. Wireless gaming devices also allow you to play games farther away from your computer.

GAMEPAD

A gamepad is a hand-held controller that you operate with both hands. This device usually offers directional controls as well as buttons you can program to perform certain functions. The buttons on a gamepad should be positioned so you can easily reach and manipulate the buttons with your fingers.

Gamepads are ideal for people who like to play games that involve a lot of action, such as sports and adventure games. Some gamepads offer force feedback, which helps to further enrich the gaming experience. For example, if you are playing a football game and someone tackles you, the gamepad may shake.

JOYSTICK

A joystick is a controller that features a lever and buttons you can use to control the movement of objects in computer games. Joysticks are commonly used for flight simulation games.

Joysticks often offer many interesting features, including throttle control, force feedback and an 8-way hat switch. The throttle control feature gives you superior control over an engine's speed and acceleration and is ideal for playing flight simulation games. Force feedback helps to create a more realistic feel when playing

computer games. For example, the joystick may shake if your airplane crashes into the ground. The 8-way hat switch feature lets you view many different angles from one standpoint. For example, while sitting in an airplane's cockpit, you would be able to view 360 degrees from your vantage point.

Joysticks also usually include buttons you can program to perform specific functions and may also include triggers which allow you to fire weapons in many games.

RACING WHEEL

You can use a racing wheel when playing driving games to create a more realistic driving experience. A racing wheel is similar to a steering wheel in a car and often includes gas and brake foot pedals for accelerating and stopping, as well as a gear shifter which allows you to change gears while driving. Racing wheels also often have buttons you can program to perform certain functions, such as activating turbo boost.

To further enhance the driving experience, racing wheels often include the force feedback feature, which provides a more realistic feel to the game. For example, if your car crashes or is side-swiped, the racing wheel may vibrate.

SCANNER

A scanner is a device that reads images and text from paper into a computer.

SCANNER APPLICATIONS

Scan Images

You can scan images, such as photographs and drawings, into a computer. You can then use the scanned images in documents, presentations and Web pages or e-mail the images to friends and family members. Most scanners come with image editing software, which allows you to change the appearance of a scanned image, such as removing red-eye from a photograph.

Scan Documents

You can scan documents to store them electronically on your computer. You can then quickly access documents on your computer and e-mail them to friends and colleagues. Most scanners come with Optical Character Recognition (OCR) software, which places scanned text into a document that you can edit in a word processor.

FLATBED SCANNER

Using a Flatbed Scanner

Most scanners are flatbed scanners. Like using a photocopier, you place images or documents you want to scan face down on the surface of a flatbed scanner. Flatbed scanners can scan flat objects such as photos and documents, thick objects such as a book and portions of oversized objects such as maps and charts. A flatbed scanner may be horizontal or vertical. Vertical flatbed scanners take up less space on your desk. Most new flatbed scanners connect to a computer through a USB (Universal Serial Bus) or FireWire connection.

Vertical Scanner

Horizontal Scanner

SCAN RESOLUTION

The resolution of a scanner determines the amount of detail a scanner can detect and is measured in dots per inch (dpi). A higher resolution results in more detailed images. The resolution of a scanner is often expressed with two numbers, such as 2400 x 2400 dpi, which define the number of dots a scanner can detect across and down one square inch.

The resolution may also be expressed with only one number, such as 300 dpi, which defines the number of dots a scanner can detect both across and down one square inch.

A resolution of 300 dpi is sufficient for images you will print, while 72 dpi is adequate for images you will display on a monitor, such as on a Web page.

COLOR DEPTH

The color, or bit, depth of a scanner indicates the number of colors a scanner can detect and is measured in bits. The higher the color depth, the higher the quality of the scanned images. You should buy a scanner capable of at least 16.7 million colors (24-bit). In addition, you should look for a scanner capable of at least 256 shades of gray (8-bit) if you plan to scan many black-and-white photos or images.

SCANNER FEATURES

• Most scanners can scan documents that measure 8.5 by 11 inches, but some scanners offer a larger maximum scan size.

• Some scanners include an automatic document feeder that allows you to scan multiple pages unattended.

• Some scanners allow you to scan transparencies, slides and film negatives.

• If you plan on scanning a lot of images or documents, look for a fast scanner. The speed of a scanner may be indicated in seconds per page.

• Scanners often come with one-touch buttons that allow you to instantly perform a task, such as scan or e-mail a scanned document.

An MP3 player is a small, portable, lightweight device that you can use to store and play music. An MP3 player allows you to listen to your favorite songs wherever you go.

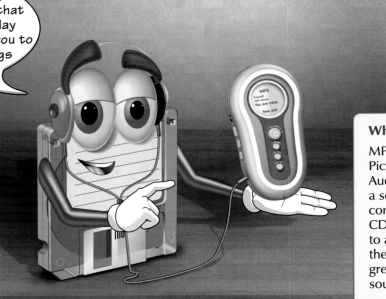

An MP3 player can store anywhere from about 15 songs (64 MB) to 25,000 songs (100 GB).

An MP3 player is also known as a digital audio player. An MP3 player that can store over 500 songs is also known as a jukebox.

The iPod made by Apple is currently the most popular MP3 player.

What is MP3?

MP3 stands for Motion Picture Experts Group Audio Layer 3. MP3 is a sound format used to compress the size of CD-quality music files to about 10 percent of their original size without greatly reducing the sound quality of the files.

PLAY OTHER TYPES OF SOUNDS

Many MP3 players can play sound files other than MP3 files, including WMA (Windows Media Audio), WAV (Waveform Audio) and Audible, which is an audio-book sound format. Although MP3 files are the most widely available type of file on the Internet, WMA files are becoming increasingly more popular. WMA files of the same quality as MP3 files are half the size, which allows you to store twice as many WMA songs on an MP3 player.

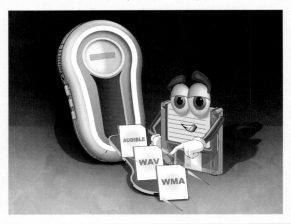

MP3 PLAYER CONTROLS

MP3 players usually have a small screen and a set of controls that allow you to choose the songs you want to play, create customized playlists, adjust the volume, display the amount of battery life remaining and more. Less expensive MP3 players may offer fewer controls.

TYPES OF MP3 PLAYERS

Memory

Many MP3 players use flash memory, which is a type of memory that you can erase and re-record onto and which does not need a power source to retain information. MP3 players with flash memory offer up to 4 GB of storage space, which allows you to store about 1,000 songs. MP3 players that use flash memory are very small and do not have any moving parts, which makes them less likely to break down and ideal to use when exercising since the music will not skip.

Media Used to Store Memory

An MP3 player can have built-in flash memory or use flash memory stored on a memory card or flash drive. When an MP3 player uses flash memory stored on a memory card, you can buy extra memory cards and store different kinds of music on each card. For example, one memory card could store your favorite rock songs, while a second card could store your favorite jazz songs.

Hard Drive

Many MP3 players have a built-in, miniature hard drive, which provides much more storage space than MP3 players that use flash memory. You can buy MP3 players with a hard drive that offer up to 100 GB or more of storage space, which can store about 25,000 songs. MP3 players with a hard drive are larger and more expensive, but are ideal for storing and playing music on long trips. MP3 players with a hard drive have moving parts, so the players are not ideal to use when exercising since the music can skip.

MP3 PLAYER

HEADPHONES

Most MP3 players come with headphones, which allow you to listen privately to your music. Good quality headphones can make a major improvement in the quality of sound an MP3 player can deliver. MP3 players usually come with inexpensive headphones, so you may want to buy higher-quality headphones that offer better sound quality. You can buy regular-sized headphones or small, lightweight headphones, called earbuds, which are ideal to use when exercising.

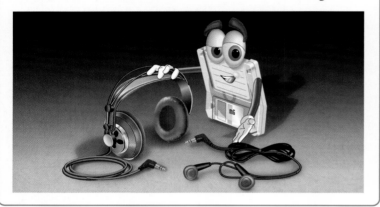

POWER SOURCE

MP3 players are powered by regular or rechargeable batteries, which typically last from 5 to 15 hours. Most MP3 players have an AC adapter that allows you to plug the MP3 player into an electrical outlet to preserve battery power when you are not on the go. If your MP3 player uses rechargeable batteries, plugging the MP3 player into an electrical outlet also allows you to recharge the batteries.

EXTRA FEATURES

Some MP3 players come with a built-in FM tuner that allows you to use your MP3 player to listen to the radio. MP3 players can also include a built-in microphone so you can make voice recordings, as well as games that you can play while listening to music. You can also obtain an MP3 player that comes with a built-in alarm clock so you can wake up to music and a sleep timer so you can fall asleep to music.

USE FOR STORAGE

MP3 players can also be used to transfer information, such as photos, presentations and data files, between computers at home, at work or on the road. You can also use MP3 players to back up important files on a computer.

OBTAIN MP3 FILES

Internet

Many companies on the Web allow you to download, or copy, individual songs or entire CDs to your computer for a small fee. Buying music on the Internet is less expensive than buying music at music stores. Each song you purchase usually costs less than $1 per song or $10 for an entire album. Popular companies that offer music include Apple (www.itunes.com), eMusic (www.emusic.com) and Napster (www.napster.com).

Music CDs

You can copy all of your favorite songs on your music CDs onto your computer. You can then transfer the songs to your MP3 player.

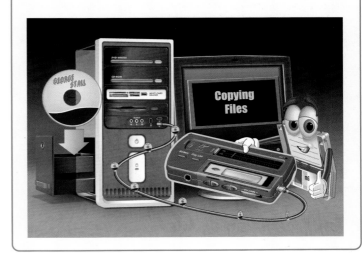

CONNECT AN MP3 PLAYER TO A COMPUTER

Using a Cable

When you want to transfer music from your computer to an MP3 player, you can use a cable to connect the MP3 player to your computer's USB (Universal Serial Bus) or FireWire port. Once you have transferred music to the MP3 player, you can disconnect the player from the computer and enjoy the music on the MP3 player. Some new MP3 players can connect wirelessly to a computer, which allows you to transfer songs without using any cables.

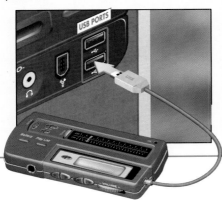

Using a Memory Card or Flash Drive

If an MP3 player has a removable memory card, you can insert the card into your computer's memory card reader. If an MP3 player has a removable flash drive, you can plug the flash drive into your computer's USB port. If an MP3 player has a built-in flash drive, you can plug the MP3 player directly into your computer's USB port. Once you have transferred music to the memory card or flash drive, you can re-insert the card or flash drive into the MP3 player to enjoy the music on the player.

DIGITAL CAMERA

A digital camera allows you to take photographs that you can easily use and work with on your computer.

WORK WITH PHOTOGRAPHS

Most digital cameras come with image editing software, which allows you to view and edit the photographs on your computer. Image editing software allows you to perform tasks such as removing red eye and removing parts of a photo you do not want to include, known as cropping. You can also purchase more sophisticated image editing software, such as Adobe's Photoshop Elements and Corel's Paint Shop Pro Studio, to work with your photographs.

PRINT PHOTOGRAPHS

If you want prints of the photographs you take, you can have the prints developed by any store you would normally take a roll of film to. You can also e-mail photograph files to companies on the Web and receive your prints in the mail.

If you want to print your own photographs, you can purchase a photo printer. Printing photographs on a photo printer can give you professional-looking prints.

TYPES OF DIGITAL CAMERAS

Point and Shoot

Point and shoot cameras are inexpensive, lightweight and can take high-quality photographs. Some point and shoot cameras are small enough to carry on a key chain. The type of lens in a point and shoot camera determines the quality of photographs the camera can produce. Higher quality point and shoot cameras use a glass lens, while lower quality cameras may use a plastic lens.

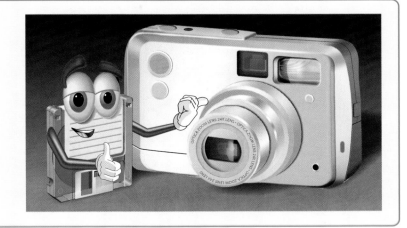

Digital SLR

Digital Single Lens Reflex (SLR) cameras produce the highest-possible quality photographs and are the most expensive type of digital camera. You can add a variety of different lenses to a SLR camera, from macro lenses for close-up shots to zoom lenses for far-away shots. You can also add an external flash component to produce better pictures in low-light situations. High-end SLR cameras are often referred to as "prosumer" cameras.

Devices With a Built-in Digital Camera

Many types of devices have built-in digital camera capabilities, including cell phones, Personal Digital Assistants (PDAs) and digital camcorders. The quality of photographs taken on these devices is generally not as good as photographs taken on a digital camera that is specifically designed to take pictures.

DIGITAL CAMERA FEATURES

Megapixels

The quality of photographs a digital camera can produce depends on the amount of detail the camera can detect. The amount of detail is measured in megapixels, which stands for millions of picture elements.

The higher the number of megapixels a camera can detect, the clearer and more detailed the photographs. Generally, the size of the prints you want for your

photographs determines how many megapixels you should use to take pictures. Most digital cameras allow you to change the megapixel settings to suit your needs. For example, if you plan to produce 4x6 prints, use a 2-megapixel setting. If you want to produce 8x10 prints, use a 5-megapixel setting on your digital camera.

Memory

Many digital cameras use flash memory, which is a type of memory that you can erase and then store more photographs on. The amount of memory offered by a digital camera is measured in megabytes (MB). The more memory a digital camera offers, the more photographs you will be able to take before you run out of space. On average, 1 MB of memory can store one or two high-resolution photographs.

A digital camera can have built-in flash memory or use flash memory stored on a memory card that you can insert and remove from the camera. When a digital camera uses flash memory stored on a memory card, you can buy extra memory cards and store photographs on one card while you continue to take more photographs on another card.

Zoom

Higher quality digital cameras include optical zoom, which uses the camera's lens to physically move closer to the subject of the photograph. Some lower quality digital cameras offer only digital zoom, which digitally enlarges the image after the photograph is taken. Cameras with optical zoom produce higher quality photographs than cameras with digital zoom.

LCD Screen

Most digital cameras come with a color LCD (Liquid Crystal Display) screen. You can use the LCD screen to preview photographs you are about to take and view photographs you have already taken. Before purchasing a camera, try viewing the screen in bright light or sunlight, since some LCD screens may appear washed out in bright light.

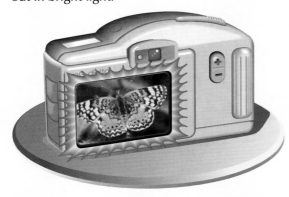

Connection Type

To transfer photographs from a digital camera to your computer, you can use a cable to connect the camera to your computer's USB (Universal Serial Bus) or FireWire port.

If a digital camera has a removable memory card, you can insert the card into your computer's memory card reader. Once you have transferred the photographs to your computer, you re-insert the card into the digital camera so you can continue taking photographs.

Batteries

Most digital cameras use rechargeable lithium-based batteries. The batteries in a digital camera may last for 100 photographs or more, depending on the camera features you use, such as the flash. You should purchase a spare battery for your digital camera and make sure you always have the battery charged and with you.

Video-Recording Capability

Some digital cameras allow you to record short videos. The length of a video you can record depends on the amount of memory your camera has. Videos recorded with a digital camera tend to be low-quality.

DIGITAL CAMCORDER

A digital camcorder is a handheld video camera that you can use to record video.

You can purchase camcorders in various sizes and weights. Smaller and lighter camcorders are more portable and comfortable to use, which is especially useful if you plan to bring your camcorder with you when traveling.

VIEWFINDER

The viewfinder is the small window you can look through on a camcorder when recording video. The viewfinder can display a black-and-white or full color image. Using the viewfinder instead of the flip-out screen will save battery life and may be easier to view when recording in bright light.

SCREEN

Most camcorders have a full color, Liquid Crystal Display (LCD) screen, which allows you to see a video you are recording or playing back. Camcorder screens typically measure between two and four inches diagonally. Better screens will rotate and flip forward for more flexibility when viewing video. Some screens are touch-sensitive, which allows you to access controls such as a fast forward or rewind button by touching the screen. Make sure you view the screen in bright light, since some screens show a better picture in bright light than others.

IMAGE STABILIZATION

Many camcorders offer an image stabilization feature which minimizes the shakes in videos due to movements of the camcorder operator.

HOW VIDEO IS STORED

Tape

Most camcorders store video on 4mm tapes, known as Mini DV (Digital Video) tapes. These tapes are widely available and can typically store about an hour of video. Some larger camcorders store video on 8mm tapes, known as Digital8 tapes. These tapes are double the size of Mini DV tapes.

You use a tape the same way you use a standard cassette tape. You need to rewind or fast forward the tape to reach the location you want to play, which can take some time and can quickly drain the battery. Tapes can also wear down over time.

DVD

Some camcorders have a DVD drive built-into the camcorder, allowing you to record information onto miniature, recordable DVDs. Most new DVD players and computers will be able to play the videos you record. With DVD camcorders, you have instant access to video because there is no need to fast forward or rewind the video to reach the location you want to play.

Memory Card

Some camcorders store video on a removable memory card. These camcorders are more expensive, but are very small and offer the best battery life. Camcorders with memory cards offer instant access to video because there is no need to fast forward or rewind the video to reach the location you want to play. A video recorded using a camcorder with a memory card is often lower-quality than a video recorded using a camcorder with a different storage type.

DIGITAL CAMCORDER

BATTERY

Camcorders run on a rechargeable battery, which can typically power a camcorder for one or two hours. Some tasks, such as rewinding or using the flip-out screen, can quickly drain a battery. You can recharge a battery by connecting a camcorder to an electrical outlet.

For long recording sessions, you can bring an extra battery. If a camcorder uses a battery that attaches to the outside of a camcorder, you can buy a higher capacity battery, which can allow for a longer recording time but may add significant weight to a camcorder.

NIGHT RECORDING

Some camcorders can emit an invisible light that allows you to record video at night or in low lighting situations. You can usually only use this feature to record video up to ten feet away. Videos you record often have a greenish tint.

TAKE PICTURES

Some camcorders allow you to take photographs, just like a digital camera. However, photos taken with a camcorder are generally of lower quality than photos taken with a digital camera. Camcorders usually store photos on a removable memory card.

CHARGE COUPLED DEVICE

A camcorder's recording quality depends on several factors relating to the Charge Coupled Device (CCD), which is a chip inside a camcorder that is used to record video.

✓ A camcorder with three CCDs will produce higher quality video than a camcorder with only one CCD.

✓ Larger CCD sizes will result in higher quality video. Typically, CCDs are between 1/6 and 1/3 inches in size.

✓ More CCD pixels will result in higher quality video.

ZOOM

A camcorder's zoom feature allows you to take closer shots. The higher the zoom number, the closer a camcorder can zoom in. Most camcorders offer optical and digital zoom. Optical zoom uses the camcorder's lens to magnify the picture, which gives you the best picture quality. Digital zoom digitally magnifies the picture shown in the lens. Digital zoom allows you to zoom in closer, but the more you zoom in, the more the picture quality degrades. You should base your buying decision on a camcorder's optical zoom.

HIGH-DEFINITION

High-definition (HD) camcorders offer more than double the video quality of standard camcorders. HD camcorders are physically bigger and more expensive than standard camcorders.

TRANSFER VIDEO TO A COMPUTER

When you want to transfer video from a camcorder to a computer, you can use a cable to connect the camcorder to a computer's FireWire port. If a camcorder stores video on a removable memory card or a DVD, you can insert the card or DVD into a computer's memory card reader or DVD player. Once you have transferred video to a computer, you can view and work with the video on the computer.

VIDEO EDITING SOFTWARE

You can use video editing software on a computer to turn video you have recorded into entertaining movies complete with edits, transitions, music and narration. Basic video editing software comes with the latest versions of Windows and Mac OS. You can obtain more sophisticated video editing software, such as Adobe Premiere Pro or Apple Final Cut Pro, at computer stores.

BLUETOOTH WIRELESS DEVICES

Bluetooth wireless technology allows computers and devices to communicate without cables.

Bluetooth was named after a tenth-century Danish king named Harald Bluetooth.

ABOUT BLUETOOTH DEVICES

Bluetooth devices use radio signals to transmit information. These devices can operate over a distance of up to 33 feet and can transmit information through barriers, such as a wall, desk or briefcase. Bluetooth devices run on batteries, which can be rechargeable.

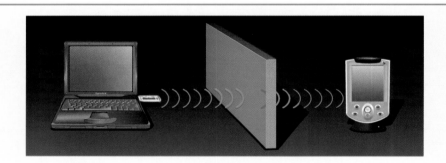

ADD BLUETOOTH TO A COMPUTER

Your computer and devices must both support Bluetooth in order to communicate wirelessly. Computers do not usually come with Bluetooth wireless capability. To add Bluetooth wireless capability to a computer, you can connect an external Bluetooth adapter, or transceiver, to a computer through a Universal Serial Bus (USB) connection.

Some Bluetooth devices, such as a mouse, come packaged with a Bluetooth adapter that adds Bluetooth capability to a computer. Once you add Bluetooth capability to a computer, any Bluetooth device can communicate with the computer.

COMMON BLUETOOTH DEVICES

Mouse, Keyboard or Headset

You can use a Bluetooth mouse, keyboard or headset to reduce clutter on your desk so you can use your desk space more efficiently. Bluetooth wireless devices also give you the flexibility to work in a more comfortable position, such as the ability to sit further away from a computer.

Cell Phone

You can wirelessly exchange information between a Bluetooth cell phone and a notebook computer. When traveling, you can dial-up your Internet service provider on a Bluetooth cell phone and use the cell phone to allow your notebook computer to connect to the Internet.

Printer

You can use a Bluetooth printer to print photos displayed on a Bluetooth cell phone. You can also use a Bluetooth printer to print documents stored on a desktop computer.

PDA

You can transfer information wirelessly between a Bluetooth Personal Digital Assistant (PDA) and a computer. When you use a PDA, you will regularly want to update information, such as e-mail messages, an appointment calendar and contact information, to ensure your PDA and computer always contain the most up-to-date information. Bluetooth makes synchronizing your PDA and computer a simple task.

NON-BLUETOOTH WIRELESS DEVICES

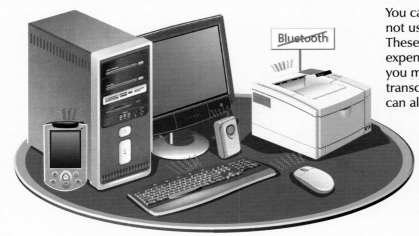

You can buy wireless devices that do not use Bluetooth wireless technology. These wireless devices tend to be less expensive than Bluetooth devices, but you may need a separate adapter, or transceiver, for each device. The devices can also be more difficult to set up.

CHAPTER 3

PROCESSING

Are you wondering how a computer operates and processes information? Find out in this chapter.

MEMORY

Memory, also called Random Access Memory (RAM), temporarily stores data inside a computer.

A computer's main memory works like a blackboard that is constantly overwritten with new data. The data stored in memory disappears when you turn off the computer.

MEMORY SPEED

The speed at which data is stored and accessed in memory is called memory speed. Memory speed is usually measured in megahertz (MHz) or gigahertz (GHz). When adding memory to your computer, make sure the memory speed is compatible with the speed of the motherboard. Most motherboards can support memory with a speed of up to 1 GHz.

MEMORY SIZE

The amount of memory determines the number of programs a computer can run at once and how fast programs will operate. Memory is measured in megabytes (MB) or gigabytes (GB). You should buy a computer with at least 512 MB of memory.

Increasing the amount of memory in your computer is one of the easiest ways to improve a computer's performance. The capabilities of the computer's motherboard determine the amount of memory you can add.

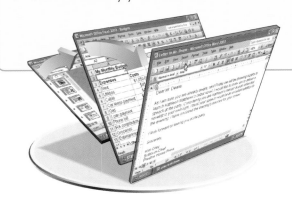

MEMORY CHIPS

Memory chips make up the main memory in a computer. The computer's motherboard determines the type of memory chip that is required.

Synchronous Dynamic RAM (SDRAM) is found in many entry-level computers and is suitable for basic computer tasks.

Double-Data-Rate Synchronous Dynamic RAM (DDR SDRAM) is faster than SDRAM and is better for working with media, such as viewing full-screen video and playing complex games.

DDR SDRAM-II, or DDR2, is a newer version of DDR SDRAM that operates even faster than the original version.

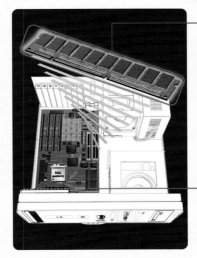

Memory Module

A memory module is a circuit board that holds memory chips. Most new computers use Dual In-line Memory Modules (DIMMs). DIMMs usually work in pairs, so when adding more memory, you should add two DIMMs that have the same amount of memory and memory speed for best results.

Memory Slot

A memory slot is a socket on the motherboard where you plug in a memory module. Most new computers come with at least two memory slots.

VIRTUAL MEMORY

If you have limited memory or you have many programs open, your computer may need to use part of the hard drive to simulate more memory, which is called virtual memory. Virtual memory significantly slows down your computer and puts more wear and tear on the hard drive.

ROM AND EPROM

Unlike RAM, Read-Only Memory (ROM) stores data that is permanent and cannot be changed. For example, ROM stores instructions that help prepare the computer for use each time you turn on the computer.

Erasable Programmable ROM (EPROM) is similar to ROM, but the data can be changed. EPROM contains data such as your user settings and the date.

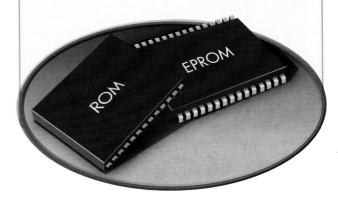

CPU

The Central Processing Unit (CPU) is the main chip in a computer.

The CPU processes instructions, performs calculations and manages the flow of information through a computer system. The CPU performs billions of calculations every second.

The CPU is also called the processor or microprocessor.

CPU COMPLEXITY

Imagine a road map of the United States printed on a fingernail and you can imagine the complexity of a CPU. The elements in a CPU are measured in microscopic units called microns or nanometers (nm). Today, elements in a CPU can be less than 0.13 microns or 100 nanometers wide. Smaller CPU elements are better because more elements can fit on a CPU. The more elements on a CPU, the faster the CPU can process information.

DUAL-CORE DESIGN

Many computer manufacturers are moving toward a dual-core design for CPUs. A dual-core design allows a computer to use two processors within a single CPU, which substantially improves the speed and power of a computer.

CHOOSE A CPU

The CPU is the primary component in a computer that affects the speed of a computer. When choosing a CPU, there are several factors you should consider.

Manufacturer

The most popular CPUs for personal computers are made by Intel and AMD (Advanced Micro Devices). Intel CPUs are more widely used, but AMD CPUs provide similar performance and usually cost less.

Generation

Each new generation of CPUs is more powerful than the generation before. Newer CPUs can process more instructions at once than older CPUs.

Speed

Each type of CPU is available in several speeds. The CPU speed is a major factor in determining how fast a computer operates. The faster the speed, the faster the computer operates. The speed of a CPU is commonly measured in gigahertz (GHz), or billions of cycles per second.

Bit Processing

Most CPUs can process 32 bits of information at a time. These CPUs are referred to as 32-bit processors and function most efficiently when used with 32-bit operating systems, such as Windows XP. Some new CPUs can process 64 bits of information at a time. Since 64-bit operating systems and applications are currently not available for Windows, 64-bit processors currently do not provide enhanced performance over 32-bit processors. 64-bit operating systems and applications for Windows will be available in the near future.

INTEL CPUS

Intel Celeron

Intel's Celeron CPU is an inexpensive CPU designed to meet the needs and budgets of most home computer users. Celeron CPUs are ideal for people who need a computer to perform basic tasks, such as exchanging e-mail, managing household finances, completing homework and playing basic games. Celeron CPUs are available with speeds up to 2.8 GHz.

A newer version of the Celeron processor, called the Intel Celeron D, offers similar performance and speeds, but is designed using newer technology.

Intel Pentium 4

The Intel Pentium 4 processor offers the speed and power required by most business computer users. Pentium 4 CPUs are ideal for people who spend their time browsing the Web, editing images, creating multimedia presentations and playing basic games. Pentium 4 CPUs are available with speeds up to 2.8 GHz.

Intel Pentium 4 with HT Technology

The Intel Pentium 4 with HT (Hyper-Threading) Technology is a CPU best suited to computer users who require a fast computer to perform tasks such as image editing and working with digital music and video. Hyper-threading technology allows the CPU to perform multiple tasks at the same time more efficiently. Pentium 4 CPUs with HT Technology are available with speeds up to 3.6 GHz.

Intel Pentium 4 Extreme Edition with HT Technology

The Intel Pentium 4 Extreme Edition CPU with HT (Hyper-Threading) Technology is ideal when using demanding applications, watching movies and playing high-end, realistic games. This CPU uses the hyper-threading technology to perform multiple tasks at the same time more efficiently. Pentium 4 Extreme Edition CPUs with HT Technology are available with speeds of 3.2 to 3.46 GHz.

AMD CPUS

AMD Sempron™

The AMD Sempron™ CPU is a low-priced processor that is ideal for people who need a computer to perform basic tasks, such as exchanging e-mail, managing household finances, completing homework and playing basic games. The AMD Sempron CPU is available in various model numbers, from 2200+ to 3100+. The higher the model number, the better the performance of the processor.

AMD Athlon™ XP

The AMD Athlon™ XP CPU was specifically designed to work with the Windows XP operating system. This CPU is suitable for business and home computer users who want a processor that is capable of working with music and video, as well as playing 3-D games.

The model number of an Athlon XP CPU refers to the approximate equivalent speed of a Pentium 4 CPU. For example, an Athlon XP 3400 CPU provides about the same performance as a 3.4 GHz Pentium 4 CPU.

AMD Athlon™ 64

The AMD Athlon™ 64 CPU is a 64-bit processor. This CPU can efficiently run 32-bit operating systems and applications and is also ready to take advantage of 64-bit programs in the future. The AMD Athlon 64 CPU is ideal for people who work with digital music and video. AMD Athlon 64 CPUs are available in various model numbers, from 3000+ to 4000+. The higher the model number, the better the processor's performance.

AMD Athlon™ 64 FX

AMD's Athlon™ 64 FX CPU is a 64-bit processor designed to give gamers and power users the computer performance they crave. This CPU is ideal for running today's realistic games and demanding high-end applications, but is also ready to handle future 64-bit applications and operating systems. The AMD Athlon 64 FX is available in three models—FX-51, FX-53 and FX-55.

MEMORY CACHE

Memory cache speeds up a computer by storing data the computer has recently used.

There are three levels of memory cache (pronounced "cash")—
L1 cache,
L2 cache and
L3 cache.

Higher-priced computers generally provide better performance because their CPUs include more and faster cache than lower-priced computers.

L1 CACHE

When a computer needs data, the computer first looks in the L1 cache. L1 cache is a small amount of very fast, very expensive memory on the CPU chip and provides the fastest way for the computer to get data. Computers usually have between 8 and 128 kilobytes (KB) of L1 cache.

L2 CACHE

If a computer cannot find the data it needs in the L1 cache, the computer looks in the L2 cache. L2 cache is often found on the CPU chip, but may also be found on the motherboard of the computer. L2 cache on the CPU chip is much faster than L2 cache on the motherboard. Computers usually have between 128 kilobytes (KB) and 1 megabyte (MB) of L2 cache. Accessing L2 cache is usually half as fast as accessing L1 cache.

L3 CACHE

When L2 cache is on the CPU chip, the computer will also often include L3 cache. L3 cache is found on the motherboard between the CPU chip and the main memory (RAM) of the computer. L3 cache is most commonly found on high-end computers used for desktop publishing, database work or games. High-end computers may have up to 2 megabytes (MB) of L3 cache. Accessing L3 cache is usually half as fast as accessing L2 cache.

RAM

If a computer cannot find the data it needs in the L1, L2 or L3 cache, the computer must get the data from the slower main memory, called RAM. The computer places a copy of the most commonly requested data from RAM in the memory cache. This process constantly updates the memory cache so it always contains the most recent and most often used data. Accessing RAM is usually about half as fast as accessing L3 cache.

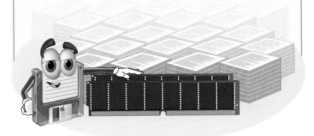

USING MEMORY CACHE

Using memory cache is similar to working with documents in your office. When you need information, you look for information in a specific, logical order. Each step along the way takes up more of your valuable time.

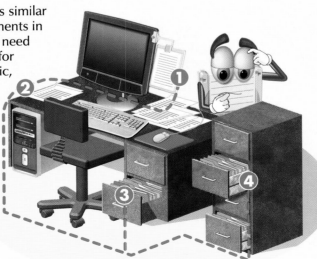

❶ Look through the document on your document holder (L1 cache).

❷ Look through documents on your desk (L2 cache).

❸ Look through documents in your desk drawer (L3 cache).

❹ Look through documents in your filing cabinet (RAM).

Working without memory cache would be similar to the time-consuming task of looking through the filing cabinet each time you need information.

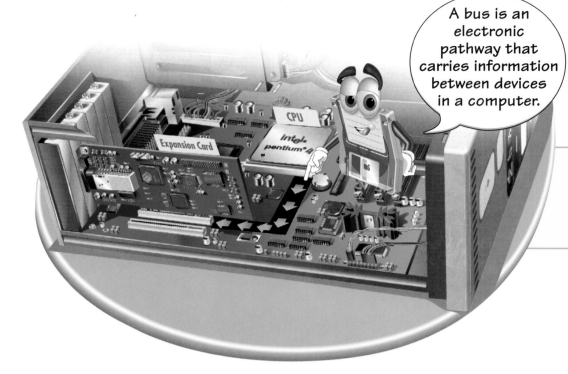

A bus is an electronic pathway that carries information between devices in a computer.

For example, a bus is used to carry information betweeen the CPU and expansion cards.

BUS WIDTH

Bus width is similar to the number of lanes on a highway. Larger bus widths can transfer more data along the bus at a time. Most types of buses measure the bus width in bits, such as 32 or 64 bits. Some types of buses measure the bus width in the number of lanes, such as 32 lanes.

BUS SPEED

Bus speed is similar to the speed limit on a highway. The higher the bus speed, the faster data travels along the bus. Bus speed is measured in megahertz (MHz), which is millions of cycles per second, or gigahertz (GHz), which is billions of cycles per second.

BUS BANDWIDTH

Bus bandwidth is a measure of the approximate amount of data a bus can transmit per second. Bus bandwidth is usually measured in megabytes per second (MB/s) or gigabytes per second (GB/s).

BUS TYPES

PCI Bus

In many computers, the Peripheral Component Interconnect (PCI) bus is the pathway between most types of devices. All the devices using a PCI bus must share the available width, speed and bandwidth of the same bus. A computer usually has only one PCI bus. PCI-X is a newer, faster version of the PCI bus.

AGP Bus

An Accelerated Graphics Port (AGP) bus is designed to carry complex graphics data between an AGP video card and the computer's memory. A computer usually has only one AGP bus. AGP is currently available in 4x, 8x and 16x speeds.

PCI Express Bus

In new, high-end computers, the PCI Express (PCIe) bus is the pathway between most types of devices. The PCIe bus provides each device with a dedicated bus, so devices do not have to share the bus. Each PCIe bus is made up of one or more lanes that transfer information in both directions at the same time. An x followed by a number in a PCIe bus name indicates the number of lanes the PCIe bus has. For example, a PCIe x16 bus has 16 lanes.

Front Side Bus

In most computers, the Front Side Bus (FSB) is the pathway between the CPU and the memory. The faster the Front Side Bus, the faster data is delivered to the CPU. A computer normally has one Front Side Bus for each CPU.

COMPARING BUS TYPES

Bus Type		Bus Width	Bus Speed	Bus Bandwidth
PCI	PCI	32 or 64 bits	Up to 66 MHz	Up to 133 MB/s
	PCI-X	32 or 64 bits	Up to 266 MHz	Up to 2 GB/s
AGP	AGP 4x	32 or 64 bits	Up to 264 MHz	Up to 1 GB/s
	AGP 8x	32 or 64 bits	Up to 533 MHz	Up to 2 GB/s
	AGP 16x	32 or 64 bits	Up to 1.08 GHz	Up to 4 GB/s
PCI Express	PCIe x1	1 lane	2.5 GHz	Up to 250 MB/s in each direction
	PCIe x32	32 lanes	2.5 GHz per lane	Up to 8 GB/s in each direction
Front Side		32 or 64 bits	Up to 1.25 GHz	Up to 10 GB/s

CHAPTER 4

STORAGE DEVICES

What is a hard drive? What is the difference between a CD-ROM drive and a CD-RW drive? Learn about storage devices in this chapter.

HARD DRIVE

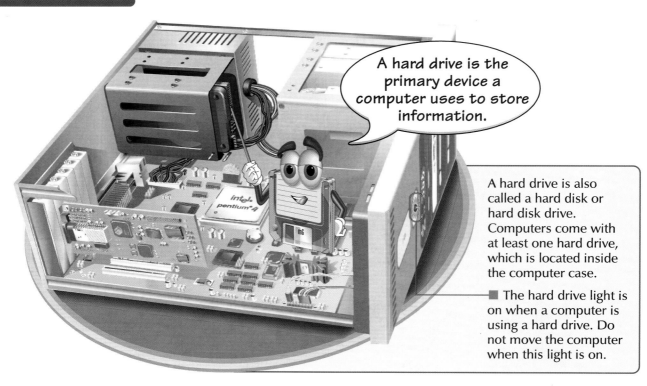

A hard drive is the primary device a computer uses to store information.

A hard drive is also called a hard disk or hard disk drive. Computers come with at least one hard drive, which is located inside the computer case.

■ The hard drive light is on when a computer is using a hard drive. Do not move the computer when this light is on.

INSIDE A HARD DRIVE

A hard drive magnetically stores data on a stack of rotating disks, called platters. The disks are stored inside the hard drive's case for protection. Several read/write heads read and record data on the disks. A hard drive also has a controller, which is a circuit board inside the hard drive that controls the hard drive.

HARD DRIVE CONTENTS

A hard drive stores data files and program files. Data files include document, image, sound and video files. Program files include the operating system, such as Windows XP and Mac OS X, and application files, such as Word and Excel. When you buy a new program, you must install, or copy, the program files to your hard drive before you can use the program. You can obtain programs on a CD, DVD or the Internet.

REASONS FOR BUYING A NEW HARD DRIVE

More Storage

Most people buy a new hard drive to provide more storage space on a computer. Hard drives are roughly doubling in storage capacity every 18 months, which means you can buy a much larger hard drive every few years. Buying a new hard drive is less expensive than buying a new computer.

Back Up Data

You can buy an external hard drive to store backup copies of files stored on a computer. Backing up data provides extra copies of files in case the original files are lost or damaged or if you accidentally change or delete files. Using a second hard drive to back up data is useful when you regularly back up a large amount of information.

Archive Data

You can copy old or rarely used files from your computer to an additional, external hard drive. You can then remove the files from your computer to free up storage space. Using an additional hard drive to archive data is useful when archiving a large amount of information.

Hard Drive Failure

If your hard drive fails, buying a new hard drive will be less expensive than buying a new computer. Before you buy a new hard drive, you can take your hard drive to a computer specialist to see if they can fix the hard drive or at least recover the data on the drive. If your computer is more than a few years old, consider buying a new computer.

CHOOSING A HARD DRIVE

Internal Hard Drive

An internal hard drive is a unit that sits in a drive bay inside a computer. An internal hard drive is less expensive than an external hard drive, but is more difficult to set up. All computers come with at least one internal hard drive.

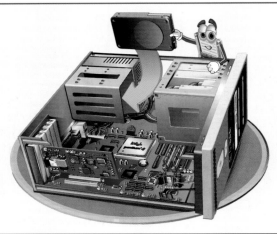

Most internal hard drives connect to a computer through an ATA (Advanced Technology Attachment) connection, which is also known as EIDE (Enhanced Integrated Drive Electronics). ATA is available in various speeds, such as ATA/100 and ATA/133. The number indicates the number of megabytes per second (MB/s) of data the connection can transfer.

External Hard Drive

An external hard drive is a unit that connects to the front or back of a computer. An external hard drive takes up room on your desk, but is easy to set up and can be moved and used with more than one computer. Most external hard drives connect to a computer through a USB (Universal Serial Bus) or FireWire connection.

Storage Capacity

The amount of information a hard drive can store is measured in gigabytes (GB). A hard drive with a capacity of 100 to 200 GB will suit most home and business users. You should purchase the largest hard drive you can afford since your files will quickly fill a hard drive. For example, an hour of DVD-quality video takes about 2 GB of hard drive space.

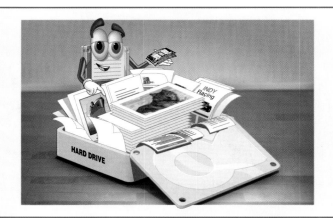

Speed

The speed of a hard drive is measured in two ways.

Revolutions Per Minute

The speed at which the platters in a hard drive spin is measured in Revolutions Per Minute (RPM). The higher the RPM, the faster the hard drive can retrieve and record data on the platters. Most hard drives have a speed of 7,200 RPM.

Average Seek Time

The speed at which a hard drive finds data is referred to as the average seek time, or average access time. The average seek time is measured in milliseconds (ms). Most hard drives have an average seek time of less than 10 ms. The lower the average seek time, the faster the hard drive can find data.

Cache

A hard drive has a cache, which is an area of memory inside a hard drive where the computer temporarily stores data recently retrieved from the drive. A cache is also known as a buffer.

When a computer needs data from a hard drive, the computer first looks in the cache. The cache can supply data thousands of times faster than the hard drive.

Each time a computer accesses data on a hard drive, the computer places a copy of the data in the cache. This allows the computer to constantly update the cache so the cache always contains the data most recently retrieved from the hard drive.

The amount of cache inside a hard drive is measured in megabytes (MB). Hard drives usually have a cache of 2, 8 or 16 MB.

BACK UP DATA ON A HARD DRIVE

Back Up Data

You should make backup copies of files stored on a hard drive to provide extra copies in case the original files are lost or damaged. You can place backup copies of files on recordable CDs or DVDs, tape cartridges or an external hard drive. Most people should back up their hard drive every day.

Backup Programs

Most operating systems include a backup program, which helps you make backup copies of files stored on a hard drive. You can also purchase a backup program, such as Retrospect (www.dantz.com) or WinBackup (www.liutilities.com), which can offer more features. Some companies on the Internet, such as BackUp Solutions (www.backuphelp.com) and Xdrive (xdrive.com), allow you to backup your files over the Internet for a fee.

Tips for Backing Up

• You can set a backup program to run automatically, which allows you to schedule a backup at night when you are not using your computer.

• You can perform two main types of backups. A full backup will back up all of your files. An incremental backup will back up only the files you have changed since the last backup. An incremental backup saves you time and storage space when backing up a lot of information.

• You do not need to back up the programs stored on a computer. You can simply use the original program discs to re-install a program at any time.

• Store your backed up files in another location to protect the files in case of fire or theft.

PROTECT AGAINST VIRUSES

A virus is a program that disrupts the normal operation of a computer. A virus can cause a variety of problems, such as the appearance of annoying messages on a screen, the destruction of information on a hard drive or the slowing down of a computer.

Files you receive from friends, family members or colleagues on a floppy disk or a recordable CD or DVD can contain viruses.

Files you obtain on the Internet and files sent as attachments in e-mail messages can also contain viruses.

You should use an anti-virus program, such as Norton AntiVirus (www.symantec.com) or McAfee VirusScan (www.mcafee.com), to regularly check your computer for viruses. You can also obtain free virus scans on the Web at www.bitdefender.com/scan and trendmicro.com.

DEFRAGMENT A HARD DRIVE

You can improve the performance of a computer by defragmenting the hard drive. Defragmenting a hard drive will make programs run faster and files open and save more quickly. Defragmenting a hard drive will also minimize wear and tear on a hard drive and help reduce hard drive errors.

A fragmented hard drive stores parts of each file in many different locations on the drive, so the computer must search many areas on the drive to retrieve a file.

You can use a defragmentation program to place all the parts of each file in one location, which reduces the time the computer spends locating files.

Some operating systems include a defragmentation program. For example, Windows includes the Disk Defragmenter program. You should defragment a hard drive at least once a month.

FLOPPY DRIVE

A floppy drive stores and retrieves information on floppy disks.

Most computers have one floppy drive, which is usually referred to as drive A. If your computer does not come with a floppy drive and you need to access information stored on floppy disks, you can purchase an external floppy drive that connects to your computer.

FLOPPY DISK

Floppy drives use 3.5 inch floppy disks, also known as floppies or diskettes. Inside a floppy disk is a thin, plastic, flexible disk that magnetically records information. The word floppy refers to this flexible disk. A floppy disk can store up to 1.44 megabytes (MB) of data.

Although floppy disks are inexpensive and can be used with most computers, memory cards and recordable CDs and DVDs are now more commonly used than floppy disks since you can store significantly more information on these types of storage media.

FORMATTED FLOPPY DISK

A floppy disk must be formatted before you can use the disk to store data. Formatting a disk prepares the disk for use by dividing it into **tracks** and **sectors**, which organizes the disk so the computer can store and retrieve data on the disk.

Most computers can use a floppy disk formatted on a computer running the Windows operating system, but computers running the Windows operating system typically cannot use a floppy disk formatted on a Macintosh computer.

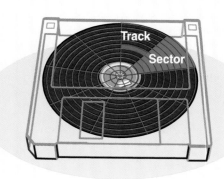

FLOPPY DRIVE APPLICATIONS

Transfer Data

You can use floppy disks to transfer data from one computer to another. This allows you to share data with friends, family members and colleagues.

Back Up Small Files

You can copy small files to floppy disks. The disks will serve as backup copies if your hard drive fails or if you accidentally erase the files.

PROTECT A FLOPPY DISK

You can prevent erasing and recording information on a floppy disk by sliding the tab to the write-protected position.

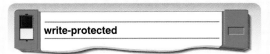

write-protected

You **cannot** erase and record information.

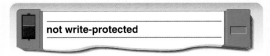

not write-protected

You **can** erase and record information.

To protect your floppy disks, make sure you keep them away from electronic devices, such as a monitor, hard drive, printer, cell phone and microwave oven, as these devices can damage the information stored on floppy disks. You should also avoid exposing floppy disks to direct sunlight and storing disks in extremely hot, cold or humid locations. For example, do not keep floppy disks in a car or a damp basement. You should also try not to spill liquids such as coffee or soda on floppy disks.

CD-ROM DRIVE

A CD-ROM drive is a device that reads information stored on Compact Discs (CDs).

Most CD-ROM drives are located inside a computer case. External CD-ROM drives that connect to a computer by a cable are also available.

CD-ROM stands for Compact Disc-Read-Only Memory. Read-only means you cannot change the information stored on discs.

CD-ROM DRIVE APPLICATIONS

Install Programs

Most programs are available on CD-ROM discs. The large storage capacity of CD-ROM discs allows you to easily install new programs on a computer.

Play Reference CD-ROM Discs

There are hundreds of CD-ROM discs available that can inform and entertain you. For example, you can buy a CD-ROM disc that offers an encyclopedia, street atlas, dictionary, guide to the human body, SAT practice tests and much more.

Play Music CDs

You can use a CD-ROM drive to play music CDs while you work on a computer. Some music CDs, called Enhanced CDs, also contain additional features you can view on your computer. For example, an Enhanced CD can include lyrics, artist interviews and music videos.

CD-ROM DRIVE SPEED

The speed of a CD-ROM drive determines how quickly information can transfer from a disc to a computer. You should buy a CD-ROM drive with a speed of at least 52x.

CD-ROM DISCS

Headphones

CD-ROM drives often have a jack at the front of the computer where you can plug in headphones. You can use headphones to listen to a disc. Headphones are useful in noisy environments or when you want to listen to a disc privately.

Storage Capacity

A CD-ROM disc is similar to the type of disc you buy at a music store. A single disc can store up to 700 megabytes (MB) of data, which is equal to an entire set of encyclopedias or over 450 floppy disks. The large storage capacity of CD-ROM discs provides a lot of room for storing files such as photographs, videos and animation.

Handle and Protect a Disc

When handling a disc, hold the disc around the edges to prevent scratching the disc.

When you finish using a disc, make sure you place the disc back in its protective case and do not stack discs on top of each other. You should also keep discs away from direct sunlight and avoid storing discs in hot locations, such as on top of a monitor or on the dashboard of a car.

CD-RW DRIVE

A CD-RW drive is a device that allows you to store information on recordable Compact Discs (CDs).

CD-RW stands for Compact Disc-ReWritable. ReWritable means you can record and erase information on discs.

A CD-RW drive, also known as a CD burner, can perform all the same functions as a CD-ROM drive, such as reading CD-ROM discs and playing music CDs.

CD-RW DRIVE APPLICATIONS

Store and Transfer Files

CD-RW drives allow you to store up to 700 megabytes (MB) of data on a single recordable CD. The large storage capacity of recordable CDs allows you to easily store and transfer files such as photographs and videos or back up copies of important files. Storing information on a recordable CD is often referred to as "burning" a CD.

Record Music

CD-RW drives allow you to create your own music CDs. You can find music on the Internet or copy music from a music CD. CD-RW drives usually come with software that allows you to record music onto a disc. You can also purchase software, such as Nero (www.nero.com), that can offer more advanced capabilities.

A single recordable CD can usually store up to 80 minutes of music or up to 10 hours of MP3 songs. Recordable CDs you create may not play in some older CD or DVD drives or players.

TYPES OF CD-RW DRIVES

Internal CD-RW Drive

An internal CD-RW drive is a unit that sits in a drive bay inside a computer. An internal CD-RW drive is generally less expensive than an external CD-RW drive, but is more difficult to set up.

External CD-RW Drive

An external CD-RW drive is a unit that connects to the front or back of a computer, usually through a USB (Universal Serial Bus) connection. An external CD-RW drive can be moved and used with other computers.

DRIVE SPEED

A CD-RW drive usually uses three numbers to indicate the speeds at which the drive performs tasks, such as 52x32x52. The first number refers to how fast the drive can read data. The second number refers to how fast the drive can record data onto a CD-RW disc. The third number refers to how fast a drive can record data onto a CD-R disc. You should buy recordable CDs that match the speed of your drive to prevent errors when recording information.

Read Speed | Record Speed on CD-RW | Record Speed on CD-R

RECORDABLE CD DISCS

A CD-RW drive can record data on a CD-R (Compact Disc-Recordable) disc only once, but can erase and re-record data on a CD-RW (Compact Disc-ReWritable) disc hundreds of times.

COMBO DRIVE

A combo drive is a drive that combines the functions of a CD-RW and DVD-ROM drive in one unit. This type of drive can read both CDs and DVDs as well as record information on recordable CDs. A combo drive takes up less room in a computer case and is less expensive than buying a CD-RW and DVD-ROM drive separately.

A DVD-ROM drive is a device that reads information stored on DVDs.

DVD-ROM stands for Digital Versatile Disc-Read-Only Memory. Read-only means you cannot change the information stored on the disc.

A DVD-ROM disc is similar in size and shape to a CD-ROM disc, but can store over six times more information. A single DVD can typically store up to 4.7 GB of information or 120 minutes of video.

Most DVD-ROM drives are located inside the computer case.

DVD-ROM DRIVE APPLICATIONS

Play DVDs and CDs

You can use a DVD-ROM drive to access information stored on DVDs, such as phone directories or maps. You can also play high quality DVD games using a DVD-ROM drive. In addition, music CDs, CD-ROM discs and recordable discs can be played on a DVD-ROM.

Play Movies

DVD-ROM drives can play DVD-Video discs, which can hold over two hours of full-length, full-screen movies. Most DVD-Video discs include a menu system, which helps you quickly go to specific scenes in a movie or access special features such as deleted scenes, alternate endings or a director's commentary. You may need to install special software on your computer to play DVD-Video discs.

DVD-ROM DRIVE SPEED

The speed of a DVD-ROM drive determines how quickly information can transfer from a disc to a computer. Current DVD-ROM drives commonly have a speed of 16x.

HANDLE AND PROTECT A DVD

When handling a DVD, hold the disc around the edges to prevent scratching the disc. When you finish using a DVD, make sure you place the disc back in its protective case and do not stack discs on top of each other. You should also keep discs away from direct sunlight and avoid storing discs in hot locations, such as on top of a monitor or on the dashboard of a car.

COMBO DRIVE

A combo drive is a device that combines the functions of a DVD-ROM drive and CD-RW (CD-ReWritable) drive into one unit. A combo drive can read both DVDs and CDs as well as record information on recordable CDs.

A combo drive takes up less room in your computer case and is less expensive than buying a DVD and CD-RW drive separately. However, if you only have a combo drive, copying information or music from one disc to another takes longer.

DVD+/-RW DRIVE

A DVD+/-RW drive is a device that allows you to store information on recordable DVDs.

DVD+RW drives are supported by companies such as Dell, Hewlett-Packard and Sony. DVD-RW drives are supported by companies such as Hitachi, Pioneer and Toshiba. Each type of drive has slightly different capabilities. A DVD+/-RW drive combines the capabilities of both types.

DVD+/-RW stands for Digital Versatile Disc+/-ReWritable. ReWritable means you can record and erase information on discs. A DVD+/-RW drive is also known as a DVD burner.

DVD+/-RW DRIVE APPLICATIONS

Read and Play CDs and DVDs

A DVD+/-RW drive can perform all the same functions as a DVD-ROM drive, such as reading DVDs, reading CDs and playing music CDs. A DVD+/-RW drive can also record information on recordable CDs and DVDs.

Store and Transfer Files

DVD+/-RW drives allow you to store up to 4.7 gigabytes (GB) of data on a single recordable DVD, which is over six times more information than a CD can store. The large storage capacity of recordable DVDs allows you to store and transfer files such as photographs, home movies or backup copies of important files. Storing information on a DVD is often referred to as "burning" a DVD.

TYPES OF DVD+/-RW DRIVES

Internal DVD+/-RW Drive

An internal DVD+/-RW drive is a unit that sits in a drive bay inside a computer. An internal DVD+/-RW drive is generally less expensive than an external DVD+/-RW drive, but is more difficult to set up.

External DVD+/-RW Drive

An external DVD+/-RW drive is a unit that connects to the front or back of a computer. An external DVD+/-RW drive takes up room on your desk, but can be moved and used with other computers. Most external DVD+/-RW drives connect to a computer through a USB (Universal Serial Bus) or FireWire connection.

DUAL-LAYER DISCS

Increased Storage

Some DVD drives can record information on special double or dual-layer (DL) discs that can store two layers of data. Dual-layer discs can store almost twice as much data as single-layer discs, but are more expensive. One dual-layer disc can store an entire Hollywood movie. All DVD players can play dual-layer DVDs.

DVD+/-RW DRIVE

DRIVE SPEED

A DVD+/-RW drive usually uses three numbers to indicate the speeds at which the drive performs tasks, such as 16x4x12. The first number refers to how fast a drive can record data onto a DVD+R (Recordable) or DVD-R disc. The second number refers to how fast a drive can record data onto a DVD+RW (ReWritable) or DVD-RW disc. The third number refers to how fast a drive can read data from a DVD-ROM (Read-Only Memory) disc.

Record Speed on a DVD+R or DVD-R disc

Record Speed on a DVD+RW or DVD-RW disc

Read Speed from a DVD-ROM disc

RECORDABLE DVDS

Types of Recordable Discs

A DVD+/-RW drive can record information onto several types of recordable DVDs. A DVD+/-RW drive can record data on a DVD+R (Recordable) or DVD-R disc only once, but can erase and re-record data on a DVD+RW (ReWritable) or DVD-RW disc hundreds of times.

DVD+R and DVD-R discs are less expensive than DVD+RW and DVD-RW discs.

Disc Storage Capacities

A DVD can be single-sided or double-sided. All DVD+/-RW drives can play and record on single and double-sided DVDs. To play or record information on both sides of a double-sided DVD, simply flip the disc over.

A DVD disc can also store one or two layers of data on each side of the disc. All DVD drives can play single and dual-layer discs, but you need a special dual-layer drive to be able to record data on dual-layer discs.

The number of recordable sides and layers a disc has determines the amount of information the disc can store. Single-sided, single-layer discs are the most commonly used type of disc.

Storage

	Single-Layer (SL)	Dual-Layer (DL)
Single-sided (SS)	4.7 GB	8.5 GB
Double-sided (DS)	9.4 GB	17 GB

RECORDABLE DVDS (Continued)

Disc Speeds

You can buy recordable DVD discs rated at different speeds, such as 8x. You should buy DVDs that match the speed of your drive to prevent errors when recording information on discs.

Protect a Disc

When labeling your DVD discs, use a felt-tip marker with a soft point to write on the top of your discs. Do not use a ballpoint pen since these pens can damage the discs.

BLUE-LASER DVD DRIVES

High-Definition Video

A blue-laser DVD drive is a new type of drive that is ideal for playing and recording high-definition video content, such as high-definition movies from a satellite dish. Blue-laser DVD drives use a blue laser, instead of the red laser used by most other DVD drives, to read and write information on discs. The blue laser is capable of storing data more densely on the disc so blue-laser DVDs have a much higher storage capacity than regular DVDs.

There are two main standards for blue-laser DVDs—Blu-ray and HD-DVD (High Definition-DVD). A Blu-ray disc can store up to 27 GB on a single-layer. An HD-DVD disc can store up to 15 GB on a single-layer.

MEMORY CARD READER

> A memory card reader is a device that records information on memory cards so you can easily transfer information between a computer and a digital device.

Popular digital devices that use memory cards include digital cameras, MP3 players, Personal Digital Assistants (PDAs) and some cell phones.

A memory card reader can be inside a computer case or connected to a computer by a cable. An external memory card reader is easy to set up and can be used with more than one computer.

MEMORY CARDS

What Is a Memory Card?

A memory card is a small card that stores information such as documents, digital photographs and music files. Memory cards, also known as flash cards, store information in flash memory. Flash memory does not need a power source to retain the information stored in the memory. Information can remain in flash memory for many years and can be erased or written over many times.

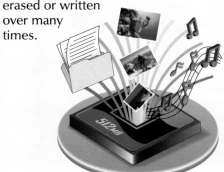

Types of Memory Cards

There are many different types of memory cards made by different manufacturers and designed for different devices. Some of the most popular memory cards are CompactFlash, Memory Stick, Micro Drive, MultiMedia Card, Secure Digital, SmartMedia and xD-Picture Card.

Care and Handling

Memory cards are more durable than other types of storage media, such as recordable CDs or floppy disks. Memory cards are small and have no moving parts, so they stand up well to being handled and transported. To protect the data on memory cards, try to avoid storing the cards in extremely hot, cold or humid locations.

MEMORY CARD APPLICATIONS

Data Transfer

Memory cards allow you to transfer information easily between computers and digital devices. For example, you can use a memory card to transfer digital photographs from your digital camera to your computer without connecting the camera to the computer. This allows you to continue using the camera while the photos are being copied to the computer.

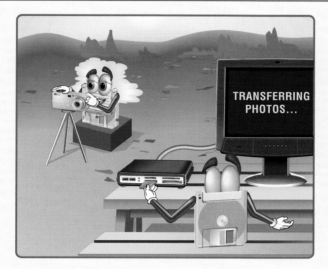

Memory cards are also ideal for transporting small to medium-size files from one computer to another. For example, if you have a report that you want to have professionally printed, you can save the report on a memory card and then deliver the memory card to a print shop.

Data Storage

Memory cards are useful for storing files. For example, you may want to remove files from a device with a limited amount of storage space, such as a PDA or notebook computer, and save the files on a memory card for later use. You can leave the files on the memory card or use the memory card to transfer the files to a desktop computer with more storage space.

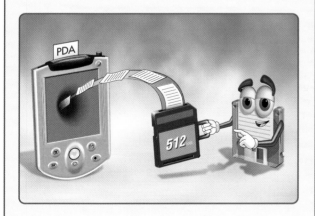

MEMORY CARD READERS

Types Available

There are as many different types of memory card readers as there are memory cards. A memory card reader may accept only one type of memory card or may have several slots that accept several different types of memory cards.

Before you purchase a memory card reader, consider what types of memory cards your digital devices use.

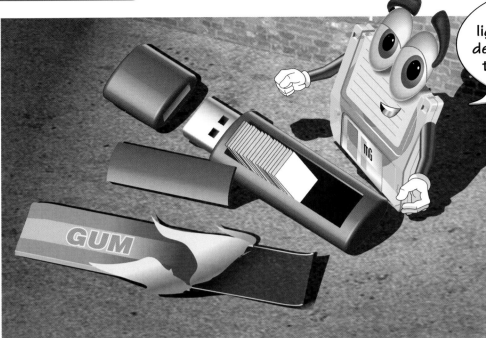

A flash drive is a lightweight storage device approximately the size of a stick of gum.

A flash drive is also known as a USB (Universal Serial Bus) key, key drive, memory key or thumb drive.

FLASH DRIVE BASICS

How Does a Flash Drive Work?

A flash drive is a device you can use to store files and transfer data between computers. To use a flash drive, you connect the flash drive to a USB port on a computer. The computer automatically recognizes the flash drive and treats the drive as an additional hard drive on the computer. You can work with and save files on the flash drive the same way you work with and save files on your computer. To transfer the files on a flash drive to another computer, you simply unplug the drive from your computer and then plug the drive into a USB port on the second computer.

Flash Memory

A flash drive stores data in flash memory. Flash memory does not need a power source to retain the information stored in memory. Data can remain in flash memory on a flash drive for up to ten years without the flash drive being connected to a power source or battery.

Flash memory is also rewritable. This allows you to add and delete data on the flash drive as often as you like.

FLASH DRIVE FEATURES

File Storage

Flash drives are ideal for storing small to medium-sized files. The drives are available in storage capacities up to 16 gigabytes (GB). Transferring data to and from a flash drive is much faster than transferring data to and from other types of removable storage, such as a floppy disk or recordable CD.

MP3 Capabilities

You can buy a device that combines the functions of a flash drive and an MP3 player. This type of device has all the features of a flash drive, but also allows you to store and play your favorite MP3 songs.

Security

Flash drives can help you keep personal information private if you share a computer with other people. You can store personal documents on the flash drive and take the documents with you when you finish using the computer.

Many flash drives also have built-in security features, such as password protection, so other people cannot access your data simply by plugging the device into their computer.

File Transfer

Flash drives are ideal for transferring files from your office computer to your home computer and back again. Many people e-mail files from one computer to another when they need to work at home, but if a file is too large to send by e-mail, a flash drive is an ideal solution. The small size and light weight of a flash drive makes it easy to transport in your pocket, on your keychain or on a strap around your neck.

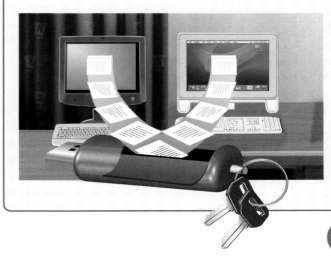

David C. Thompson
President
Dynamic Advertising Inc.
123 Lincoln Ave.
New York, N.Y.
10023

Dear Mr. Thompson,

I would like to take this opportunity to congratulate you and your company
for winning First Prize in the 2000 Logo Design Contest. It gives me the
greatest pleasure to inform you that the Judging Committee's decision was
unanimous. Your entry was clearly the best among the hundreds of
outstanding entries we received this year.

Enclosed please find a copy of the Judging Committee's report, which
states that "the logo designed by Dynamic Advertising Inc. enhances
the company's image through the creative use of colorful design
principles."

The award will be presented on August 20 at the International Design
Institute's annual banquet. We hope to see you during the presentation.

Once again, please accept my congratulations.

Sincerely,

Karen Davis
Chairperson
Judging Committee

264 Main St.
Chicago, Ill.
10487
(555) 555-1241
(555) 555-1219

CHAPTER 5

SOFTWARE

Are you ready to start writing a report or keeping track of your budget? Browse through this chapter to discover how software can help you get the job done.

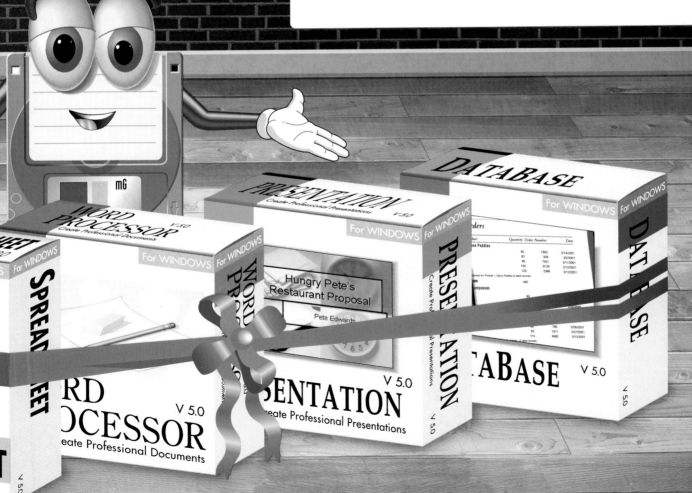

Software helps you accomplish specific tasks.

You can use software to write letters, manage your finances, edit photographs, play games and much more.

Software is also called an application or a program.

GET SOFTWARE

You can buy software at computer stores. There are also thousands of programs available on the Internet that you can purchase or download free of charge.

INSTALL SOFTWARE

Software you buy at a computer store may come on a CD-ROM disc or a DVD-ROM disc. Before you can use the software, you install, or copy, the contents of the disc onto your computer.

SOFTWARE UPDATES

New Version

When a manufacturer adds new features to existing software, the updated software is given a new name or new version number. This helps people distinguish new versions of the software from older versions.

Patch

Manufacturers also may create minor software updates, called patches, to make corrections or improvements to software. A patch is also often referred to as a service pack.

BUNDLED SOFTWARE

Bundled software is software that comes with a new computer system or device, such as a scanner. Companies often include bundled software to let you start using the new equipment right away. For example, new computer systems usually come with word processing, spreadsheet and graphics programs.

GET HELP

Most software comes with a built-in help feature and printed documentation to help you learn to use the software. You can also buy computer books that contain detailed, step-by-step instructions or visit the manufacturer's Web site for more information about the software.

WORD PROCESSOR

A word processor helps you create professional-looking documents quickly and efficiently.

Commonly used word processing programs include Microsoft Word and Corel WordPerfect.

WORD PROCESSING BASICS

Documents

You can create many different types of documents, such as letters, reports, manuals, newsletters, brochures and Web pages.

Editing

Word processors offer many features that help you work with text in documents. You can easily add, delete or rearrange text. Most word processors also allow you to check your documents for spelling and grammar errors.

Printing

You can produce a paper copy of a document. Word processors allow you to see on the screen exactly what your document will look like when printed.

WORD PROCESSING FEATURES

Formatting

Word processors allow you to easily change the appearance of text in your documents. For example, you can center text, use various fonts and create bulleted or numbered lists. You can also change the overall appearance of the pages in a document by adjusting the margin settings, adding page numbers and creating page borders.

Tables

Most word processors allow you to create a table to neatly organize the information in a document. You can enhance the appearance of a table by adding colors and borders to the table.

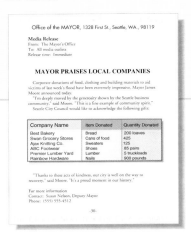

Images

Most word processors include many types of images that you can use to enhance the appearance of a document. Using images can help you draw attention to important information in a document.

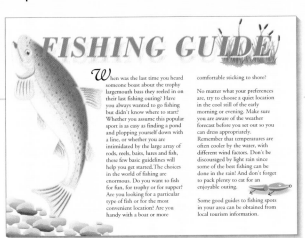

Mail Merge

Most word processors offer a merge feature that allows you to quickly produce personalized letters, envelopes and mailing labels for each person on a mailing list.

SPREADSHEET

A spreadsheet program helps you manage personal and business finances.

Commonly used spreadsheet programs include Microsoft Excel, Corel Quattro Pro and Lotus 1-2-3.

WHY USE A SPREADSHEET?

Manage Finances

You can use a spreadsheet program to perform calculations, analyze data and attractively present information such as a budget or sales report.

Manage Data in a List

A spreadsheet program allows you to store a large collection of information, such as a mailing list or product list. Spreadsheet programs include tools for organizing, managing, sorting and retrieving data.

If you want greater control over a list stored on your computer, use a database program. Database programs are specifically designed to manage lists of data.

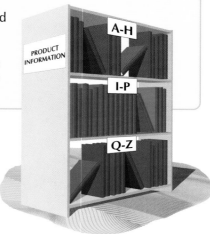

SPREADSHEET FEATURES

Editing

When working with a spreadsheet program, you can add, delete, move or copy data. Most spreadsheet programs can remember the last change you made and allow you to undo, or cancel, the change.

Formatting

A spreadsheet program offers many features that help you enhance the appearance of your spreadsheets. You can easily change the design and size of data. You can also add color and borders to the cells in a spreadsheet.

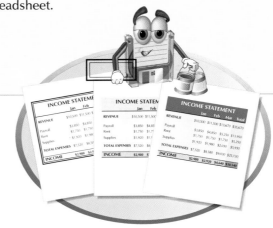

Formulas and Functions

Spreadsheet programs provide powerful formulas and functions to calculate and analyze your data. A function is a ready-to-use formula that helps you perform specialized calculations. For example, in some spreadsheet programs, the SUM function adds a list of numbers.

Charts

Most spreadsheet programs allow you to create charts to graphically display the data in a spreadsheet.

If you later change the data used in a chart, the spreadsheet program will automatically update the chart for you.

DATABASE

A database program helps you manage large collections of information.

Database programs are commonly used to manage mailing lists, phone directories, product listings and payroll information.

Commonly used database programs include Microsoft Access, Corel Paradox and FileMaker Pro.

DATABASE BASICS

Table

A table is a collection of information about a specific topic, such as a mailing list. You can have one or more tables in a database.

Address ID	First Name	Last Name	Address	City	State/Province	Postal Code
1	Jim	Smith	258 Linton Ave.	New York	NY	10010
2	Brenda	Jones	50 Tree Lane	Boston	MA	02117
3	Todd	Riley	68 Cracker Ave.	San Francisco	CA	94110
4	Chuck	Martin	47 Crosby Ave.	Las Vegas	NV	89116
5	Melanie	Fox	26 Arnold Cres.	Jacksonville	FL	32256
6	Susan	Fields	401 Idon Dr.	Nashville	TN	37243
7	Allen	Frost	10 Heldon St.	Atlanta	GA	30375
8	Greg	Best	36 Buzzard St.	Boston	MA	02118
9	Jason	Lee	15 Bizzo Pl.	New York	NY	10020
10	Jim	Patterson	890 Apple St.	San Diego	CA	92121

A table consists of fields and records.

Field

A field is a specific category of information in a table. For example, a field can contain the first names of all your clients.

Record

A record is a collection of information about one person, place or thing in a table. For example, a record can contain the name and address of one client.

WHY USE A DATABASE?

Store Information

A database stores and manages a collection of information related to a particular subject or purpose. You can efficiently add, update, view and organize the information stored in a database.

Database programs provide forms you can use to quickly change the information stored in a table.

Find Information

You can instantly locate information of interest in a database. For example, you can find all clients with the last name Smith.

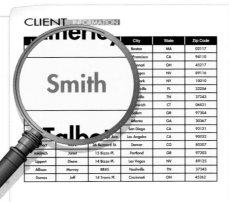

You can also perform more advanced searches, called queries. When you create a query, you ask a database program to find information that meets certain criteria, or conditions. For example, you can find all the clients living in California who purchased more than $100 of supplies last year.

Analyze and Print Information

You can perform calculations on the information in a database to help you make accurate and informed decisions.

You can neatly present the information in professionally designed reports.

An application suite is a collection of programs sold together in one package.

You can buy software at computer stores. There are also thousands of programs available on the Internet that you can purchase or download free of charge.

ADVANTAGES

Cost
Buying programs as part of an application suite costs less than buying each program individually.

Easy to Use
Programs in an application suite share a common design and are created to work together. Once you learn one program, it is easier to learn the others.

DISADVANTAGE

Since all the programs in an application suite come from the same manufacturer, you may not get the best combination of features for your needs. Make sure you evaluate all the programs in an application suite before making your purchase.

TYPES OF APPLICATION SUITES

There are many types of application suites available. Three of the most commonly used types of application suites are office, design and digital media suites.

Office Suites

Office suites contain software programs that are useful for most home and business computer users. Most office suites include a word processor, a spreadsheet program, a presentation program and a contact management program.

Many office suites also include other programs, such as a desktop publishing or database program. Microsoft Office and Corel WordPerfect Office are popular office suites.

Design Suites

Design suites contain software programs that are used for creating and editing images, Web page publishing or desktop publishing. Popular design suites include MacroMedia Studio MX and Adobe Creative Suite.

Digital Media Suites

Digital media suites contain software programs that allow you to create your own CDs and also edit photographs, music and videos to create your own DVD movies. Popular digital media suites include Apple iLife and Roxio Easy Media Creator.

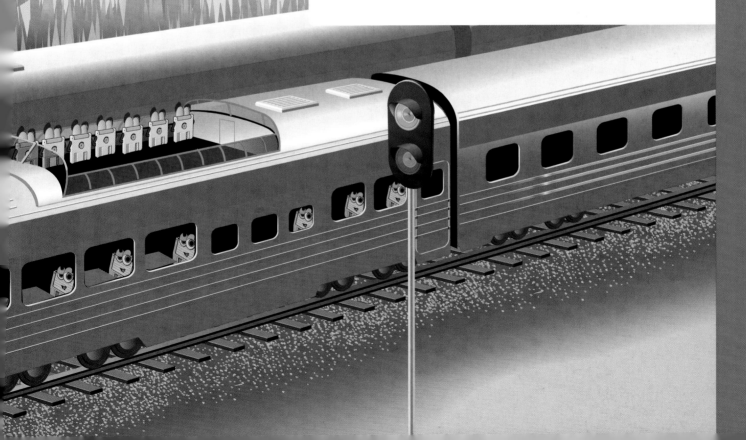

CHAPTER 6

OPERATING SYSTEMS

Are you wondering what an operating system is and which one is best for you? This chapter provides the information you are looking for.

INTRODUCTION TO OPERATING SYSTEMS

An operating system is the software that controls the overall activity of a computer.

An operating system, also called an OS, ensures that all parts of a computer system work together smoothly and efficiently.

OPERATING SYSTEM FUNCTIONS

Control Hardware

An operating system controls the different parts of a computer system, such as the hard drive, memory, monitor and printer, and enables all the parts to work together.

Run Software

An operating system runs software, such as spreadsheet, word processing, image editing and game software.

Manage Information

An operating system provides ways to manage and organize information stored on a computer. You can use an operating system to sort, copy, move, delete or view files.

TYPES OF OPERATING SYSTEMS

MS-DOS

MS-DOS stands for MicroSoft Disk Operating System. MS-DOS displays lines of text on the screen and allows you to perform tasks by typing text commands. MS-DOS was the first popular operating system, but is now rarely used.

Windows

Windows is the most popular operating system used on home and business computers. Windows is offered by Microsoft.

Linux

Linux is a powerful operating system that is available for free on the Web. There are many different versions of the Linux operating system available from many different manufacturers.

Mac OS

Mac OS is the operating system used on Macintosh computers. Mac OS is popular in the graphic arts and desktop publishing industries. Mac OS is offered by Apple.

COMPATIBILITY

An operating system can usually only run programs designed for that operating system. For example, you cannot use a program designed for Windows, such as Microsoft Word, on a computer running Linux. The type of operating system used by a computer is also known as the platform.

OPERATING SYSTEM UPDATES

Manufacturers often offer minor software updates, called patches, to make corrections or improvements to an operating system. A collection of patches is known as a service pack. You should regularly check your operating system manufacturer's Web site to obtain any available patches and service packs.

MS-DOS is an operating system that performs tasks using text commands you enter.

MS-DOS stands for Microsoft Disk Operating System.

COMMANDS

The command prompt (C:\>) tells you that MS-DOS is ready to accept a command. You enter a command to perform a task or start a program. A single command can usually tell the computer what you want to accomplish. For example, the DATE command tells the computer to display the current date. The cursor, which appears as a flashing line on the screen, indicates where the text you type will appear.

FILE NAMES

When you store a file on a computer, you must give the file a name. An MS-DOS file name consists of a name and an extension separated by a period and cannot contain any spaces. The **name** describes the contents of the file and can have up to eight characters. The **extension** identifies the type of file and consists of three characters.

FILE ORGANIZATION

Like folders in a filing cabinet, MS-DOS uses directories to organize the data stored on a computer.

The root directory (C:\) is the main directory. All other directories are located within this directory.

A path describes the location of a file.

• The path for this file is C:\letters\personal\john.let

WINDOWS 3.1

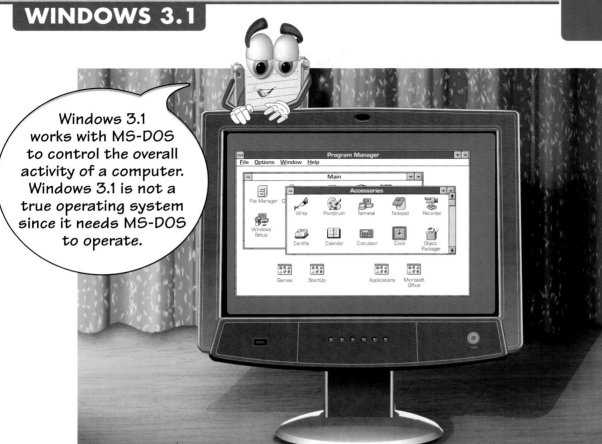

Windows 3.1 works with MS-DOS to control the overall activity of a computer. Windows 3.1 is not a true operating system since it needs MS-DOS to operate.

Windows 3.1 was first released in 1992.

WINDOWS 3.1 FEATURES

Icons

In Windows 3.1, you use a mouse to navigate the screen and choose icons to perform tasks. An icon is a small picture on the screen that represents an item on the computer. A program icon allows you to start a program, such as a word processor. A group icon contains similar program icons. For example, the Games group icon contains several games.

Windows

Windows 3.1 uses windows, or small rectangles, to display icons on the screen. For example, the Accessories window displays all the icons for the available accessory applications, such as a calendar and a calculator. Each window has a title bar that displays the name of the window.

File Management

Windows 3.1's File Manager allows you to view and organize all the files stored on your computer. Windows 3.1 uses directories to organize information, just as you would use folders to organize papers in a filing cabinet.

WINDOWS 95, 98 AND ME

Between 1995 and 2000, Microsoft released three new operating systems—Windows 95, Windows 98 and Windows Me. All three operating systems are independent operating systems because they do not need MS-DOS to operate.

Windows 95, Windows 98 and Windows Me, also known as the Windows 9x operating systems, all have a similar look and feel.

WINDOWS 95

Windows 95 is the successor to Windows 3.1.

Desktop and Taskbar

Windows 95 introduced an enhanced desktop, which is the background area of the screen. You can save files and folders on the desktop or place shortcuts on the desktop for easy access. A shortcut provides a quick way to open a document or program you use regularly.

Windows 95 also provides a taskbar at the bottom of the desktop. The taskbar contains the Start button, which lets you quickly access programs and documents, and displays the name of each open window on the screen.

— Shortcut

— Taskbar

Network Capabilities

Windows 95 includes built-in networking capabilities, such as Network Neighborhood, which allows you to view the folders and files available on your network.

WINDOWS 98

Windows 98 is the successor to Windows 95. There are two versions of Windows 98. Windows 98 SE (Second Edition) includes many enhancements and updates to the original version of Windows 98.

Internet Capabilities

Windows 98 includes several programs that allow you to view and exchange information on the Internet, including Internet Explorer and Outlook Express. Internet Explorer lets you browse through information on the Web, while Outlook Express lets you exchange electronic mail with people around the world.

FAT32

FAT32 is a file system that better manages data on large hard drives to reduce wasted space. Windows 98 can convert your hard drive to FAT32 without disrupting the programs and documents currently on your computer.

WINDOWS ME

Windows Me is the successor to Windows 98. Windows Me stands for Windows Millennium Edition.

Multimedia Capabilities

Windows Me allows you to record, edit and save videos on your computer using Windows Movie Maker. Windows Me also includes a version of Windows Media Player, which helps you manage your multimedia files and allows you to listen to radio stations over the Internet.

Restore Your Computer

If you are experiencing problems with your computer, Windows Me includes a System Restore feature which allows you to return your computer to a time before the problems occurred. For example, if you have accidentally deleted program files, you can restore your computer to a time before you deleted the files.

WINDOWS NT

Windows NT is a powerful version of the Windows operating system that provides advanced networking and security features.

Windows NT is available in two main versions.

Workstation

Windows NT Workstation is a version of the Windows NT operating system that is used on client/server and some peer-to-peer networks.

Many powerful applications are designed specifically to run on Windows NT Workstation.

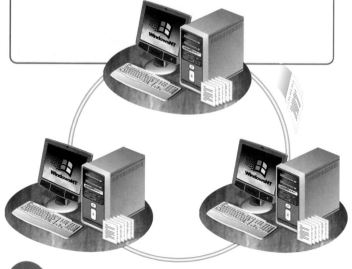

Server

Windows NT Server is a version of the Windows NT operating system that is used on client/server networks. Windows NT Server is designed to support the heavy processing demands of a network server.

The client computers on a network running Windows NT Server can use a variety of operating systems, such as Linux, Windows XP and Mac OS X.

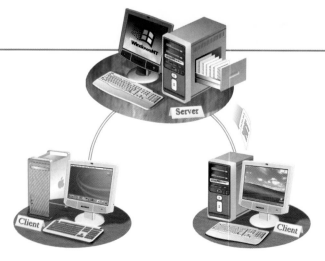

Windows 2000 is the successor to Windows NT. This operating system offers improved networking and security features.

There are several versions of Windows 2000 available.

Professional

Windows 2000 Professional is commonly used on client/server networks but can also be used on peer-to-peer networks. This operating system offers increased stability and provides tools that can help you maintain your computer. Windows 2000 Professional is intended for business use.

Server

The original versions of Windows 2000 for large client/server networks—Windows 2000 Server and Windows 2000 Advanced Server—have been replaced by Windows Server 2003. This powerful operating system is designed to support the heavy network processing demands of medium to large businesses and Internet service providers. There are several versions of Windows Server 2003 available.

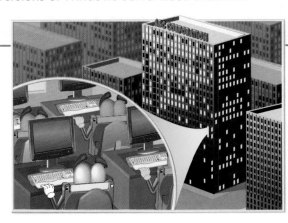

WINDOWS XP

Windows XP is the newest version of the Windows operating system. Windows XP stands for Windows eXPerience.

Windows XP has a newly designed desktop and is more stable and reliable than previous versions of the Windows operating system.

WINDOWS XP FEATURES

Multimedia Capabilities

Windows XP allows you to play music and watch DVDs on your computer as well as copy songs to a recordable CD. You can also transfer your home movies to your computer so you can organize and edit the movies before sharing them with your friends and family.

Computer Sharing

If you share your computer with other people, you can create user accounts to keep the personal files and settings for each person separate. You can also choose to keep your programs and files open while another person uses the computer. This allows you to return quickly to your programs and files after the other person finishes using the computer.

Remote Assistance

Windows XP's Remote Assistance feature allows you to ask a friend who is online at another computer to view your computer screen and chat with you to help you solve a computer problem. With your permission, the other person can even control your computer to help you fix the problem.

POPULAR WINDOWS XP VERSIONS

There are several versions of Windows XP available, including Home Edition, Professional Edition and Media Center Edition.

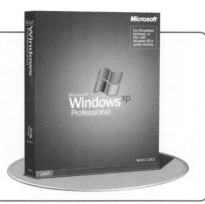

Windows XP Home Edition

Windows XP Home Edition is the successor to Windows Me and is marketed toward home users. The Home Edition includes advanced digital media features that allow you to work with digital music, photos and movies.

Windows XP Professional Edition

Windows XP Professional Edition is the successor to Windows 2000 and is ideal for business use. The Professional Edition has the same look and feel as the Home Edition, but provides more advanced features and is more reliable. The Professional Edition offers more security and privacy options than Windows XP Home Edition.

Windows XP Media Center Edition

Windows XP Media Center Edition is ideal for home entertainment use, including features that allow you to record television programs, play DVDs and organize and listen to music. This edition of Windows XP is only available with the purchase of a Media Center computer, which is specially designed for home entertainment use and includes a keyboard and a remote control.

THE FUTURE OF WINDOWS

Within the next few years, Microsoft will be launching the next version of the Windows operating system. The next version will be a 64-bit operating system, which makes it up to twice as fast as today's operating systems, most of which are 32-bit. Other upgrades to the new operating system will include improved security features and more efficient ways of saving and finding files on your computer.

Linux is a powerful, inexpensive, UNIX-based operating system.

There are many versions, known as distributions, of the Linux operating system made by different companies. Some versions of Linux are available for free on the Internet.

Linux can be difficult to install and set up, but after Linux is set up on a computer, the operating system is easy to learn and use.

OPEN SOURCE CODE

Linux is an open source code operating system. Open source code means that Linux can be copied, modified and distributed with few restrictions. This allows programmers to customize Linux to meet the individual needs of different types of computer users and networks. The flexibility of Linux is one of the reasons Linux is becoming so popular.

DESKTOP AND SERVER VERSIONS

There are versions of Linux available for desktop computers and for network servers. Linspire by Lindows and MandrakeLinux by MandrakeSoft are two popular Linux versions that are available for desktop computers. Popular versions of Linux for network servers include Red Hat Linux and SuSE Linux.

LINUX FEATURES

User Interface

When working in Linux, you can use a Graphical User Interface (GUI), such as GNOME or KDE, which displays pictures on the screen to help you perform tasks. You can also use the command line, which allows you to perform tasks by entering text commands. Working in the command line allows you to perform many tasks more quickly than in a GUI, but you must know the proper text commands.

Software

Many Linux versions include a wide variety of software, such as a drawing program, word processing program, spreadsheet program, calendar, Web browser and e-mail program. Programs made to run on other operating systems, such as Windows or Mac OS, will not usually run on a Linux computer.

Multiple Operating Systems

Many versions of Linux allow you to run Linux and another operating system, such as Windows XP, on the same computer. This is useful if you want to have the ease-of-use and flexibility of the Linux operating system, but you need to use software programs that are not available for Linux.

Multiple Users

When you install Linux, a root account and one or more user accounts are created. The root account is useful for performing administrative and maintenance tasks. User accounts are better suited to performing daily tasks. You can set up a different user account for each person who uses your computer.

MAC OS X

Mac OS X (ten) is the latest version of the Macintosh operating system.

The Macintosh operating system can only be used on Macintosh computers.

MAC OS X VERSIONS

There are currently several versions of Mac OS X. The two most recent versions are commonly known as Mac OS X Jaguar (version 10.2) and Mac OS X Panther (version 10.3).

OPERATING SYSTEM CORE

Mac OS X offers an improved operating system core, or kernel, over previous Mac OS versions, such as Mac OS 9. This improved kernel helps ensure your computer hardware and software work together efficiently and provides more stability than previous versions of the Macintosh operating system.

Mac OS X is designed to take advantage of multiple CPUs, or processors, in a computer. If your computer has more than one CPU, Mac OS X will run faster, with even more stability.

MAC OS X FEATURES

Graphical User Interface

Mac OS X offers a new Graphical User Interface (GUI) that is designed to make the operating system easier to use than previous versions, such as Mac OS 9. The new GUI features photo-quality icons and an area at the bottom of the screen, called the Dock, where you can store items, such as folders and programs, that you frequently access.

Enhanced Graphics Capabilities

Mac OS X combines several advanced graphics technologies, including Portable Document Format (PDF), QuickTime and OpenGL, to provide enhanced graphics capabilities. This improves the display of graphics in programs such as desktop publishing and games.

Manage Photos and Create Movies

You can use iPhoto to copy photos from a digital camera to your computer so you can view, organize and edit your photos. Mac OS X also includes iMovie, which allows you to transfer video from a digital camcorder to your computer so you can organize and edit the video before sharing it with friends and family.

Video Conferencing

Mac OS X includes a program called iChat, which allows you to have audio and video conversations with other people over the Internet.

THE FUTURE OF MAC OS

The next version of Mac OS X will be version 10.4, also known as Tiger. Tiger will have more than 150 new features, including a faster and more efficient method of searching for files on your computer. The new version of the Mac operating system will also include many improvements for working on the Internet and communicating with other people.

CHAPTER 7

NOTEBOOK COMPUTERS

Do you want a computer that you can take with you when you are on the go? This chapter will provide the information you need to find the notebook computer that is right for you.

A notebook computer is a small, lightweight computer that you can easily transport.

A notebook computer is also known as a portable or laptop computer.

ABOUT NOTEBOOK COMPUTERS

All the components of a notebook computer, including the keyboard, pointing device, speakers and screen, are built into one unit. This gives a notebook computer a compact design that is built to withstand movement.

You can buy a notebook computer with the same capabilities as a desktop computer. Notebook computers are more expensive than desktop computers but use less power, which helps to conserve energy.

ADVANTAGES OF NOTEBOOK COMPUTERS

A notebook computer can run on batteries, which allows you to use the computer when electrical outlets are not available, such as when traveling or outdoors. You can also use a notebook computer to easily work in every room in your house or bring work home instead of staying late at the office. Since notebook computers are small and lightweight, you can bring a notebook computer anywhere you may need to use a computer.

DESKTOP REPLACEMENT

Desktop replacements are the largest and most powerful type of notebook computer. These notebooks use top-of-the-line components, including fast processors, lots of memory, large screens and fast hard drives. Desktop replacements are ideal for individuals who need the power of a desktop computer in a portable format.

ULTRAPORTABLE NOTEBOOK

Ultraportable notebooks are thin, lightweight, energy-efficient computers that provide excellent battery life. Ultraportable notebooks are ideal for frequent travelers who are concerned about the weight of a computer.

BUDGET NOTEBOOK

Budget notebooks are ideal if you want most of the features offered by a desktop replacement, but are on a limited budget. Budget notebooks are ideal for performing everyday tasks, such as word processing, browsing the Web and exchanging e-mail.

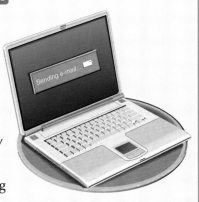

CONVERTIBLE NOTEBOOK

A convertible notebook is a notebook computer with a display that you can swivel around and collapse on top of the keyboard to turn the notebook into a slate. You can use the keyboard to enter information or use an electronic pen to write on the screen.

GAMING NOTEBOOK

A gaming notebook is ideal for playing games when traveling. Gaming notebooks include fast processors, lots of memory, large screens, fast hard drives, impressive graphics and a trendy overall design.

SLATE

A slate, or tablet, is a thin, lightweight notebook computer that you can hold under your arm like a clipboard. Slates provide most of the power and performance of a desktop computer. You use an electronic pen to write on the screen or an on-screen keyboard to enter data.

A notebook computer can run on a battery, which allows you to use the computer when electrical outlets are not available, such as when traveling or outdoors.

TYPES OF BATTERIES

New notebook computers use Lithium-Ion (Li-Ion) batteries. Some older notebook computers use Nickel Metal Hydride (NiMH) batteries. The amount of energy supplied by a battery is measured in watt-hours (WHr) or milliamp-hours (mAh). The higher the number, the longer the battery will last.

MONITOR A BATTERY

Most notebooks display information on the screen indicating the approximate amount of battery power remaining. A battery can typically power a notebook computer for only a few hours, depending on the computer's efficiency, the tasks you are performing and the capacity of the battery.

1:48 hours (66%) remaining

RECHARGE A BATTERY

When a notebook is connected to an electrical outlet, the battery will automatically recharge. You can use the notebook while the battery recharges, but the battery will recharge much faster when the notebook is turned off.

If you are unable to recharge a battery when traveling, bring an extra battery so you can work for a longer period of time. Some notebook computers allow you to insert more than one battery at a time.

Batteries slowly wear down over time. If you frequently use a notebook computer, you may want to buy a new battery every two to three years.

PORTS

Sound Ports

Sound ports allow you to connect external speakers, headphones, a microphone or an external sound source, such as a stereo system.

TV Out Port

A TV out port allows you to connect a television so you can present computer information on a larger screen.

USB Port

A Universal Serial Bus (USB) port is a high-speed port that can connect most types of devices, including a printer, mouse, joystick and MP3 player. Most new notebooks come with at least two USB 2.0 ports.

FireWire Port

A FireWire port, which is also known as an IEEE 1394 port or i.LINK port, is a high-speed port that can connect many types of devices, including a digital camcorder, external hard drive and MP3 jukebox.

Notebook computers have many ports, which are connectors that are usually located at the back or side of a computer. A port allows you to plug in an external device.

Parallel Port

A parallel port, which is also known as a printer port or LPT port, can connect an older printer or scanner.

Monitor Port

A monitor port, which is also known as a VGA port, allows you to connect a full-sized monitor or projector.

Network Port

A network port, which is also known as an RJ-45 port, allows you to connect a computer to a network or high-speed Internet connection, such as a cable modem.

Modem Port

A modem port, which is also known as an RJ-11 port, connects a modem so you can send and receive faxes from your computer and access the Internet through a telephone line.

INPUT AND OUTPUT DEVICES

There are many input and output devices you can use with a notebook computer.

POINTING DEVICES

You can use several devices to move the pointer around the screen of a notebook computer. A notebook computer has either a pointing stick, a touchpad or both built into the case. If you are looking for greater precision, you can purchase a separate mini mouse.

Pointing Stick

A pointing stick is a small device that resembles the eraser at the end of a pencil. You push a pointing stick in different directions to move the pointer on the screen. Pointing sticks also have one or more buttons, similar to mouse buttons, that you can press to perform an action such as a click. These buttons are usually located just below the bottom of the notebook's keyboard.

Touchpad

A touchpad is a surface that is sensitive to pressure and motion. When you move your fingertip across the pad, the pointer on the screen moves in the same direction. To perform an action such as a click, you can tap the touchpad or press one of the touchpad's buttons.

Mini Mouse

A mini mouse is usually about half the size of a full-size mouse, which makes it much easier to use in small spaces and when traveling. If you find a pointing stick or touchpad awkward to use, you should consider a mini mouse. A mini mouse can connect to a notebook wirelessly or may have a retractable cord that plugs into the notebook's USB (Universal Serial Bus) port.

SPEAKERS

All notebook computers come with built-in sound capabilities and speakers. To help improve the quality of sound produced by a notebook, you can connect external speakers to a notebook.

MODEM AND NETWORK CONNECTIONS

A modem allows you to access the Internet or a network at work through a telephone line. A network connection allows you to connect to a home or office network or to a high-speed Internet connection, such as a cable modem. Most notebooks come with a built-in modem and network connection.

KEYBOARD

The keys on a notebook keyboard may be small and close together to save space. Before buying a notebook, type several paragraphs of text to make sure the keyboard is suitable for you. For example, make sure you can press a single key at a time, the Spacebar is a suitable size and you can easily enter numbers.

SCREEN

Notebook computers have a built-in LCD (Liquid Crystal Display) screen. An LCD screen uses very little power, which extends the length of time you can use the notebook before needing to recharge the battery. Notebook screens are measured diagonally and usually range from 10 to 17 inches. Widescreen screens are also popular in notebooks.

With an LCD screen, you cannot change the resolution of the screen. Manufacturers usually indicate the resolution at which the screen has the sharpest display, known as the native resolution.

HARD DRIVE

The hard drive is the primary device a notebook uses to store information. The amount of information a hard drive can store is measured in gigabytes (GB). A hard drive of up to 100 GB is adequate for most notebook users. You should purchase the largest hard drive you can afford, since your files will quickly fill a hard drive.

RECORDABLE CD OR DVD DRIVE

A notebook computer may include a drive that allows you to store information on CDs, such as a CD-R (CD-Recordable) or CD-RW (CD-ReWritable) drive. Alternatively, a notebook may include a drive that allows you to store information on DVDs, such as a DVD+/-RW (DVD-ReWritable) drive.

Some notebooks include a combo drive, which combines the functions of a DVD-ROM (DVD-Read-Only-Memory) drive and a CD-RW drive in one unit to save space.

FLASH DRIVE

A Flash drive, or USB (Universal Serial Bus) key, is a small, durable, portable device that you can use to store files or transfer data between your notebook and another computer. A Flash drive connects to a notebook through a USB port.

MEMORY CARD READER

Some notebooks include a memory card reader. Memory cards allow you to transfer information easily between a notebook and a digital device, such as a digital camera, MP3 player, Personal Digital Assistant (PDA) or mobile phone. A memory card reader may be built into a notebook, may connect to a notebook using a cable or may be added through the notebook's PC Card slot.

> The CPU and the memory are the two main processing components in a notebook computer.

CPU

The Central Processing Unit (CPU) is the main chip in a computer. The CPU processes instructions, performs calculations and manages the flow of information through a computer. CPU speed is measured in megahertz (MHz) or gigahertz (GHz). Generally, the higher the number of MHz or GHz, the faster the processor can process information, but other factors, such as the design of the processor, also play a role in the performance of the CPU.

Types of CPUs

A notebook computer may use the same type of CPU found in a desktop computer, such as an Intel Pentium 4 or an AMD Athlon™ 64, or may use a mobile CPU. A mobile CPU, such as Intel Pentium M or AMD Turion™ 64 mobile technology, is specifically designed for a notebook computer. A CPU designed for a notebook computer will generally process information slower than a desktop computer CPU, but will use less battery power.

MEMORY

Memory, or RAM (Random Access Memory), temporarily stores data inside a computer. Memory works like a blackboard that is constantly overwritten with new data. A notebook computer running Windows XP should have at least 512 megabytes (MB) of memory to ensure that programs run smoothly.

Shared Memory

Many entry-level notebooks include integrated graphics instead of a video card. When a notebook has integrated graphics, the computer's memory is shared between processing information and displaying graphics, which can result in slower overall performance compared to a notebook that has a separate video card.

PC CARD

A PC Card is a thin, lightweight, credit card-sized card that adds a new capability to a notebook computer.

PC Cards are also called PCMCIA Cards, which stands for Personal Computer Memory Card International Association—the association that developed the PC Card standard.

TYPES OF PC CARDS

PC Cards are mainly available in two different sizes—Type I and Type II. Type I PC Cards are thinner than Type II Cards. ExpressCards, which will soon be available, are smaller, faster versions of PC Cards.

You insert a PC Card into a slot in a notebook computer. Many notebook computers have one or two slots.

PC CARD EXAMPLES

FireWire
A PC Card can provide one or more FireWire ports, which are high-speed ports that can connect many types of devices, including a digital camcorder, external hard drive or MP3 jukebox.

Modem
A PC Card can provide modem capabilities so you can send and receive faxes or connect to the Internet over a telephone line.

Networking
A PC Card can allow you to access a wired or wireless network.

USB
A PC Card can provide one or more Universal Serial Bus (USB) ports, which are high-speed ports that can connect many types of devices, including a printer, mouse, joystick or MP3 player.

GPS
A PC Card with a Global Positioning System (GPS) receiver allows you to determine your exact geographic location.

You can connect a notebook computer to wireless devices, such as a wireless mouse, and to a wireless network.

CONNECT TO WIRELESS DEVICES

Bluetooth Wireless Devices

Bluetooth wireless technology allows notebook computers and devices, such as a printer, to transmit information using radio signals instead of cables. Most notebook computers do not come with Bluetooth capability. You can add Bluetooth capability by adding a Bluetooth PC Card or connecting an external Bluetooth adapter, or transceiver, to a notebook through a Universal Serial Bus (USB) connection.

Other Wireless Devices

A notebook computer can also use wireless devices that do not use Bluetooth wireless technology. These devices tend to be less expensive than Bluetooth devices, but you may need a separate adapter, or transceiver, for each device and the devices can be more difficult to set up.

CONNECT TO A WIRELESS NETWORK

Wireless Network

A wireless, or wi-fi, network allows computers to share information using radio signals instead of cables. Most new notebook computers have built-in wireless networking capabilities. You can also add wireless networking capabilities to a notebook by adding a wireless networking PC Card or connecting an external wireless networking adapter to a notebook through a Universal Serial Bus (USB) connection.

Centrino

A notebook computer with the Centrino label is optimized for mobile computing. These notebooks have wireless networking capabilities built-in and provide a longer battery life, but generally have smaller screens and operate more slowly than other notebook computers.

A Personal Digital Assistant (PDA) is a portable computer that is small enough to carry in your hand. A PDA is also called a handheld computer.

PDAs can offer most of the features of a notebook computer, but also offer several advantages, including a smaller size, a lighter weight and a longer battery life. PDAs, however, include a smaller screen, are more difficult to enter text into, and are not ideal for working with large documents or for performing complex tasks.

TYPES OF PDAS

There are two main types of PDAs—Pocket PC and Palm. Both types of PDAs offer a similar design and comparable features. If you are familiar with using the Windows operating system on your desktop or notebook computer, you may want to try Microsoft's Pocket PC since this device has a similar look and feel to Windows. Palm, however, offers more software to choose from and a wider range of models and prices.

PDA APPLICATIONS

When choosing a PDA, look at the features the PDA offers. Each PDA will offer a different set of features. You can use a PDA to view and work with documents, store contact information, manage appointments, create to-do lists and set alarms.

You can also use a PDA to browse the Web, exchange e-mail messages, play music and videos, display pictures and play games. A PDA can also allow you to make a voice recording so you can take notes while on the road.

Some PDAs can include a built-in cell phone or digital camera. PDAs may also allow you to add a Global Positioning System (GPS) receiver, which allows you to determine your exact geographic location.

SCREEN

Larger PDA screens provide a larger viewing area, but take up more space, which makes them less portable.

Most PDAs offer a full-color display. Low-end PDAs may offer a black-and-white or one-color display, such as a blue-and-white display.

Display Resolution

The size of a screen is indicated by the display resolution, which is the number of horizontal and vertical dots, called pixels, on a screen. Look for a display resolution of at least 320 x 240.

Bright Light

Most PDAs offer a backlit display, which can help you more clearly see the screen in poor or bright lighting. For a superior screen display in bright light conditions, look for a PDA with a transflective display.

Cool Features

Some PDA screens will automatically adjust from a portrait to landscape orientation when you turn the device. You can also obtain PDAs with screens that slide out of the device to make the device more compact.

BATTERY

PDAs run on a rechargeable battery. A battery can typically power a PDA for several hours, depending on the tasks you are performing and the brightness level you have set for the screen. PDAs can indicate the approximate amount of battery power remaining. You can recharge a battery by connecting a PDA directly to an electrical outlet or by placing a PDA in its cradle, which directly connects to an electrical outlet.

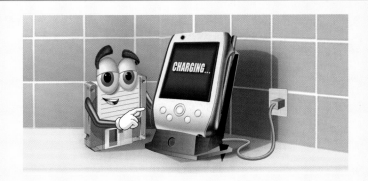

PERSONAL DIGITAL ASSISTANTS

INPUT INFORMATION

PDAs have a touch-sensitive screen. You use an electronic pen, called a stylus, to select objects on the screen and input information. The stylus usually slides into the device for safekeeping. Most PDAs also include handwriting-recognition software, which allows a PDA to interpret and enter information you write on the screen.

Keyboard

When you want to enter text into a PDA, you can use the on-screen keyboard. Some PDAs come with a built-in keyboard located below the screen and many PDAs allow you to connect a small keyboard to the device. PDAs usually allow you to connect a full-sized keyboard, which can often collapse to save space when traveling.

MEMORY

PDAs include flash ROM (Read-Only Memory) to store programs and files, and use built-in RAM (Random Access Memory) to process information. The amount of memory is measured in megabytes (MB). High-quality PDAs will offer a minimum of 64 MB each of built-in flash ROM and RAM.

PDAs usually come with at least one memory card slot, which allows you to insert a memory card. You can use a memory card to store additional information.

64 MB Flash ROM
64 MB RAM

PROCESSOR

The processor, or Central Processing Unit (CPU), is the main chip in a PDA. The processor in a PDA processes instructions, performs calculations and manages the flow of information through a PDA.

The speed of a processor is measured in megahertz (MHz). The higher the number of MHz, the faster the processor can process information. Look for a PDA with a processor speed of at least 400 MHz.

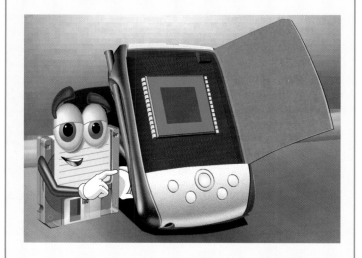

CONNECT TO THE INTERNET

You can use a PDA to connect to the Internet to browse the Web and send and receive e-mail messages.

Using a Cell Phone

If a PDA has a built-in cell phone, you can use the cell phone to dial-up your Internet service provider and connect to the Internet. If a PDA does not have a built-in cell phone, you can connect the PDA to an external cell phone to connect to the Internet.

Wi-fi Hotspot

Hotspots

If a PDA has built-in wi-fi, or wireless networking, capability, you can use a wi-fi hotspot to connect the PDA to the Internet. A wi-fi hotspot is a public place, such as a coffee shop, hotel or airport, which allows people to connect to the Internet through a wireless network set up on their premises.

SYNCHRONIZE INFORMATION

You can synchronize information between a PDA and a computer at home or at work. Synchronizing information ensures your PDA and computer always contain the most up-to-date information. You may want to update information such as documents, e-mail messages, an appointment calendar and contact information.

Updating Appointments...

CONNECT WIRELESSLY TO OTHER DEVICES

Most PDAs come with wireless capability, which allows a PDA to communicate with other devices without using any cables. A PDA with wireless capability can wirelessly connect to devices such as a keyboard, headset, cell phone, printer and computer. Most PDAs come with infrared wireless capability, which uses a beam of light. Some PDAs come with Bluetooth wireless capability, which uses radio signals.

CHAPTER 8

MACINTOSH COMPUTERS

Are you wondering what a Mac is? This chapter introduces you to Macintosh computers.

INTRODUCTION TO MACINTOSH COMPUTERS

Macintosh computers, also known as Macs, were introduced by Apple Computer in 1984.

Macintosh computers were the first home computers with a mouse, on-screen windows, menus and icons.

MACINTOSH ADVANTAGES

Easy to Set Up and Use

Macintosh computers are easy to set up, which allows you to quickly get started using a new Macintosh computer. The graphical interface of a Macintosh makes this type of computer easy to work with.

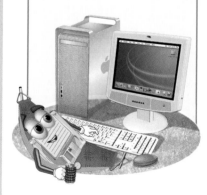

Music, Video and Desktop Publishing

The Macintosh computer is widely used in the music, video and desktop publishing industries, so it is finely tuned to handle processing large amounts of information quickly and efficiently.

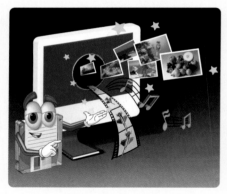

In a home environment, the sound and video capabilities of the Macintosh make the computer ideal for working with multimedia. For example, you can easily create DVD movies from your home videos and create your own music CDs.

Compatibility

The latest Macintosh computers are compatible with PCs, which gives you a lot of flexibility. Many programs that were written for the PC can be run on the Macintosh. You can also connect a Macintosh computer to a network with other Macs or PCs.

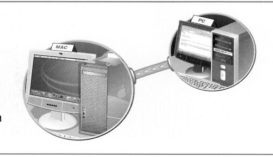

OPERATING SYSTEM

GUI

Like the Windows operating systems, the Macintosh operating systems use a Graphical User Interface (GUI). A GUI allows you to use pictures instead of text commands to perform tasks.

Many Macintosh computers use the Mac OS X (ten) operating system, which offers advanced Internet, sound and video features.

Mac OS X is a 64-bit operating system, which means the operating system can accomplish tasks and process information much faster than 32-bit operating systems such as Windows XP and Mac OS 9.

The current main versions of Mac OS X are Mac OS X Jaguar (version 10.2) and Mac OS X Panther (version 10.3). The next version of Mac OS X will be version 10.4, also known as Tiger.

CPU

The Central Processing Unit (CPU), also known as a processor, is the main chip in a computer. A CPU processes instructions, performs calculations and manages the flow of information through a computer system. Today's Macintosh computers use the PowerPC G4 or PowerPC G5 CPU.

PowerPC G4

The PowerPC G4 processor is available with speeds up to 1.5 gigahertz (GHz) and is currently used in the iBook and PowerBook notebook computers as well as the eMac.

PowerPC G5

The PowerPC G5 processor is a 64-bit processor, which means it is much faster than the 32-bit processors used in most computers. The PowerPC G5 processor is available with speeds up to 3.0 gigahertz (GHz) and is currently used in the iMac and Power Mac computers.

PROFESSIONAL COMPUTERS

Apple Computer's Power Mac G5 is currently the most powerful type of Macintosh computer.

The Power Mac G5's processing speed and power make it an ideal computer for professionals who work in the music, video and publishing industries and frequently perform graphics-intensive tasks.

DUAL PROCESSOR

The Power Mac G5 computer uses two PowerPC G5 processors to provide increased processing speed and power. Using dual processors is useful for people who work with programs that require high processing capabilities, such as desktop publishing and image creation programs.

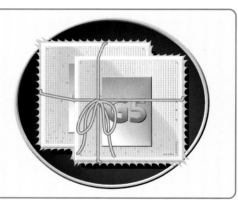

MULTIMEDIA

The Power Mac G5 provides advanced multimedia capabilities. For example, the Power Mac G5 comes with video editing software and can easily accommodate high-speed devices, such as a digital camcorder. The Power Mac G5 also has plenty of processing power, enabling the computer to work easily with high-quality, full-screen, full-motion video.

ADD NEW DEVICES

You can easily add new devices to a Power Mac G5 to expand the capabilities of the computer as your needs increase. For example, if you need to add more memory to improve the computer's performance, a Power Mac G5 can accommodate up to 8 gigabytes (GB) of memory. A Power Mac G5 also has several FireWire ports that you can use to connect new devices. For example, you could connect an external hard drive using any of the computer's FireWire ports.

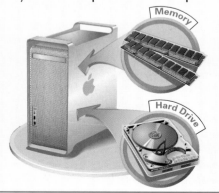

The iMac G5 is a Macintosh computer that is designed to meet the needs of most home and office computer users.

The iMac G5 is an all-in-one computer that contains components such as speakers, a hard drive, CD-RW drive and DVD-R or DVD-ROM drive all within a two-inch thick LCD (liquid crystal display) monitor.

UNIQUE DESIGN

The iMac G5's unique design makes it easy for new computer users to set up and use. All you have to do is attach the keyboard and mouse, plug in the computer and turn it on. In addition, the all-in-one design of the iMac G5 is ideal for wireless computing. You could hang the monitor on a wall and use a wireless keyboard and mouse to reduce the clutter on your desk.

SOFTWARE

The iMac G5 comes with software that home users will find useful. For example, you can use the iMovie and iDVD programs to create and edit home movies and then burn the movies onto a DVD disc. You can also use the Quicken program included with the iMac G5 to manage your personal finances.

INTERNET ACCESS

The iMac G5 comes with a built-in modem and software you can use to access the Internet. These features can help you quickly get started browsing pages on the Web and communicating with other people on the Internet.

BUDGET COMPUTERS

Apple offers two inexpensive, yet powerful computers. The eMac and Mac mini computers are designed to meet the needs of home users and students.

The eMac and Mac mini computers both currently use the PowerPC G4 processor.

eMAC

The eMac is an all-in-one computer that contains components such as a monitor, hard drive, speakers and rewritable CD drive all in a single unit. Since all the components of the eMac are located in one unit, the computer does not take up much space on a desk.

The eMac is ideal for students and home users who want to get up and running quickly, without having to spend a lot of time connecting components and learning how to use a new computer.

MAC MINI

The Mac mini is a tiny, yet powerful computer. This computer is only 6.5 inches wide, 2 inches tall, and weighs less than 3 pounds. The Mac mini comes with most of the components and software you would find in a full-size Macintosh computer, but in a smaller package and at a fraction of the price.

The Mac mini comes with a hard drive, a modem and a combo drive, which combines the capabilities of a rewritable CD drive and DVD drive. A regular Macintosh monitor, mouse and keyboard plug into the Mac mini, but are sold separately.

INPUT AND OUTPUT DEVICES

Modem

A modem allows you to send and receive faxes from your computer and access the Internet through a telephone line. Most Macintosh computers come with a built-in modem.

There are many input and output devices you can use with a Macintosh computer.

Monitor

A monitor displays text and images generated by a computer. Most new Macintosh computers come with an LCD (liquid crystal display) monitor.

Printer

A printer produces a paper copy of documents you create on a computer. When buying a printer for a Macintosh computer, make sure the printer is Macintosh-compatible. A printer designed for a PC may not work with a Mac.

Imaging Device

You can purchase an imaging device, such as a scanner, camcorder or digital camera, for your Macintosh computer. A scanner reads images and text into a computer, while a camcorder or digital camera allows you to transfer videos or pictures to your computer.

Keyboard

The keys on a keyboard let you enter information and instructions into a computer. Some new Macintosh computers allow you to connect a keyboard to a computer wirelessly.

Speakers

Speakers play sound generated by a computer. All Macintosh computers come with built-in high-quality sound capabilities.

Mouse

A mouse is a handheld pointing device that lets you select and move items on your screen. A Macintosh mouse has only one button. Some new Macintosh computers allow you to connect a mouse to a computer wirelessly.

A port is a connector at the back or front of a computer where you plug in an external device.

Sound Ports

Sound ports allow you to connect speakers, a microphone and an external sound source, such as a stereo system.

Modem Port

A modem port connects a modem so you can send and receive faxes from your computer and access the Internet through a telephone line.

Monitor Port

A monitor port connects a monitor.

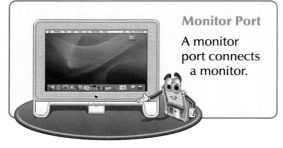

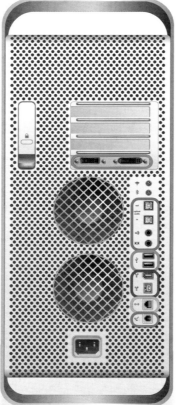

USB Port

A Universal Serial Bus (USB) port is a high-speed port that can connect most types of devices, including a mouse, keyboard, printer and MP3 player. Most new Macintosh computers come with at least two USB 2.0 ports.

FireWire

A FireWire port is a high-speed port that allows you to connect many devices that require fast data transfer speeds, including a digital camcorder, iPod and external hard drive. New Macintosh computers come with at least one FireWire 400 port.

Ethernet (Network) Port

An Ethernet (network) port allows you to connect a computer to a network or a high-speed Internet connection.

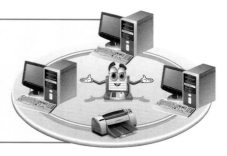

NOTEBOOK COMPUTERS

The iBook and PowerBook Macintosh notebooks are small, lightweight and easy to transport.

Like other notebook computers, the iBook and PowerBook come with a built-in keyboard and screen. The latest iBook and PowerBook notebooks use the PowerPC G4 processor.

iBOOK

The iBook is an affordable notebook computer that is designed to meet the needs of most home computer users. You can use the iBook to browse the Web, play games, exchange e-mail, play CDs and DVDs and create documents. The iBook weighs less than six pounds, has either a 12.1-inch or 14.1-inch screen and can provide up to six hours of battery life.

POWERBOOK

The PowerBook is a powerful notebook computer that is ideal for business use. The PowerBook is great for users who want the size of a portable computer with the power of a desktop computer.

The PowerBook is compatible with PCs, so you can easily connect the notebook to a PC or Mac network at your office. Weighing in at less than seven pounds, the PowerBook has a 12, 15 or 17-inch screen and can provide up to five hours of battery life.

CHAPTER 9

NETWORKS

Do you wonder how multiple computers can share information efficiently? Learn about wired and wireless networks in this chaper.

INTRODUCTION TO NETWORKS

A network is a group of connected computers that allows people to share information and equipment.

Share Equipment

Computers connected to a network can share equipment, such as a printer. Sharing equipment allows companies to save money since several people on the network can use the same equipment.

Share Information

A network allows you to easily share information with other people. Sharing information on a network is especially useful when people on a network are working together on a project and need to access the same files.

TYPES OF NETWORKS

Local Area Network

A Local Area Network (LAN) is a network that connects computers that are usually located in the same building. A LAN can connect from as few as two computers to several hundred computers.

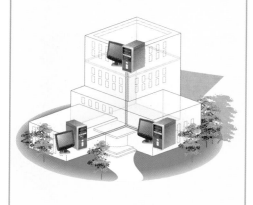

Metropolitan Area Networks

A Metropolitan Area Network (MAN) is a network that connects two or more local area networks in the same city.

Wide Area Network

A Wide Area Network (WAN) is a network that connects two or more local area networks or metropolitan area networks across the country or world. When a single company owns and controls a wide area network, the WAN is often referred to as an enterprise network. The Internet is the largest wide area network.

NETWORK ADVANTAGES

Exchange E-Mail

You can exchange e-mail messages with other people on a network. Larger companies often set up a mail server that only people on the network can use, which offers a faster, more secure and more flexible e-mail service.

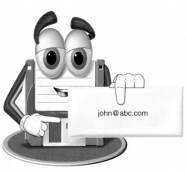

Work Away From the Office

When traveling or at home, you can connect to the network at work to access information on the network and retrieve e-mail messages.

Exchange Instant Messages

Networks allow you to send messages that will instantly appear on other computer screens on the network. Since instant messages appear immediately, they are ideal for messages that require attention right away.

Collaborate

Networks make it easy to collaborate on a project. You can use software on a network to help schedule meetings, have more than one person work on the same document and much more.

Share an Internet Connection

Computers on a network can share a single Internet connection.

Videoconferencing

Networks can allow you to have face-to-face conversations with other people on the network located across the city or country.

NETWORK HARDWARE

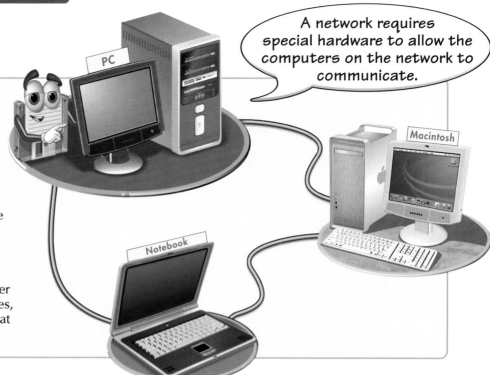

A network requires special hardware to allow the computers on the network to communicate.

Computers

A network can connect different types of computers, such as PC and Macintosh computers, as well as desktop and notebook computers.

Computers usually come with networking capabilities built into the motherboard. Some computers are equipped with a Network Interface Card (NIC), which is an expansion card inside a computer that offers networking capabilities. If a computer does not have networking capabilities, you can add a NIC to the computer at any time.

Cables

Cables are the wires that physically connect computers and equipment on a network. There are two main types of cables that are used on a network—twisted pair and fiber-optic.

Twisted pair cable is the most commonly used cable and is available in several different categories. Each category supports a different speed, which is measured in megabits per second (Mbps).

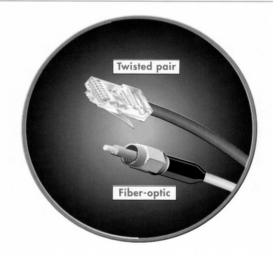

Fiber-optic cable is an expensive type of cable, but it can carry information significantly faster and over longer distances than twisted pair cable. Fiber-optic cable is also less susceptible to interference and is more secure since others cannot eavesdrop on the cable. Since fiber-optic cable can transmit information at a near infinite speed, you will never need to upgrade fiber-optic cable.

Type of Cable		Speed
Twisted Pair	Category 5 (CAT-5)	100 Mbps
	Category 5e (CAT-5e)	1,000 Mbps
	Category 6 (CAT-6)	10,000 Mbps
Fiber-optic		Near Infinite

Router

A router is a device that determines the route, or path, along which information is transferred on a network. A router is often used to connect a Local Area Network (LAN) to another network or to allow every computer on a network to share one Internet connection. A router connects to a switch or hub unless the router has a built-in switch or hub that can connect all the computers on a network.

Switch or Hub

A switch or hub is a device that provides a central location where the cables from each computer or piece of equipment on a network come together. A switch or hub acts like a traffic cop, managing the flow of information on a network. When a network uses a switch, all the computers always have full-speed access to the network. When a network uses a hub, all the computers must share the speed available to the network, which means a busy network or large file transfers will slow the speed of the entire network. Most networks use a switch instead of a hub.

Ethernet

Ethernet is the most popular hardware standard used on Local Area Networks (LANs). There are several Ethernet standards and each one can exchange information on a network at a certain speed. The speed of each Ethernet standard is measured in megabits per second (Mbps). All the hardware on an Ethernet network must support the same Ethernet standard.

Ethernet Standard	Speed
Ethernet (10BaseT)	10 Mbps
Fast Ethernet (100BaseT)	100 Mbps
Gigabit Ethernet (1000BaseT)	1,000 Mbps
10 Gigabit Ethernet (10GBaseT)	10,000 Mbps

Resources

A network resource is a device that computers on a network can use. The most common type of network resource is a printer.

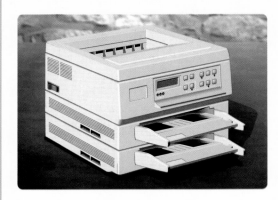

PEER-TO-PEER NETWORK

A peer-to-peer network provides a simple and inexpensive way to connect computers and is ideal for home and small office networks.

Each person on a peer-to-peer network stores their files on their own computer. Each person can access shared files stored on other computers on the network.

Manage Files

A peer-to-peer network stores files on each computer on the network, which makes the files difficult to manage, back up and protect. However, if one computer malfunctions, the rest of the network will not be affected.

Operating System

Each computer on a peer-to-peer network must use the same type of operating system, such as Windows.

Share Files

Each person on a peer-to-peer network is responsible for specifying which files they want to share.

Reduced Performance

When a computer on a peer-to-peer network shares information or equipment, the performance of the computer can be affected. For example, when a person on the network prints a document, the computer attached to the shared printer may run slower.

CLIENT/SERVER NETWORK

A client/server network provides a highly efficient way to connect computers and is ideal for larger companies and when sharing large amounts of information between computers.

Each person on a client/server network stores their files on a central computer. Everyone connected to the network can access the files stored on the central computer.

Manage Files

All the files on a client/server network are stored on the server, which makes the files easy to manage, back up and protect. However, if the server malfunctions, the entire network will be affected.

Server

A server is a powerful, central computer that stores the files of every person on a client/server network. A network can have one or hundreds of servers.

Operating System

A client/server network can connect computers using the same or different operating system, such as Windows XP and Mac OS X.

System Administrator

Client/server networks have a system administrator who manages the network. A system administrator can perform tasks such as adding new computers to the network and backing up information on the server. A system administrator is also known as a network manager or information systems manager.

Client

A client is a computer that can access information stored on a server. Most client computers are regular computers that have applications installed. In some client/server networks found in large companies, client computers are known as thin clients. In this case, the applications reside on the server and the server performs most or all of the processing.

HOME NETWORKS

If you have more than one computer at home, you can set up a network so the computers can exchange information and share equipment, such as a printer.

A home network also allows you to play multiplayer games, which allow several people to compete against each other on different computers on a network.

SHARE AN INTERNET CONNECTION

A home network allows you to share one Internet connection with all the other computers on the network. Sharing an Internet connection allows each person on a network to browse the Web, exchange e-mail messages and more. For the best performance when sharing an Internet connection on a home network, you should use a high-speed Internet connection, such as a cable modem or Digital Subscriber Line (DSL) connection. For a more efficient network setup and added security when accessing the Internet, you should also use a router, which is a device that each computer on a network connects to.

WIRED OR WIRELESS

You can connect all the computers on a home network with cables or set up a wireless network that enables computers to communicate using radio signals instead of cables. Wireless networks, which are also known as wi-fi networks, are useful when computers are located where cables are not practical or economical. Wireless networks also allow you to use a notebook computer in many locations in a home, such as in a basement or on the deck. Wireless networks can be easier for unauthorized people to access compared to wired networks.

> A network must be protected from unauthorized access to ensure the security of the information and equipment on the network.

FIREWALL

A firewall is special software or hardware designed to protect a private network from unauthorized access. Companies often use a firewall to control the information that passes between a private network and the Internet. All the information entering or leaving the network passes through the firewall, which examines the information and blocks information that does not meet the security criteria. You may notice that a firewall prevents access to certain Web sites or removes files attached to e-mail messages you receive.

USER NAME AND PASSWORD

You usually have to enter a user name and password, known as "logging on" to a network, when you want to access information on a network. Entering a user name and password ensures that only authorized people can access the information stored on a network. You should choose a password that is at least eight characters long, includes a combination of letters and numbers and does not use words that people can easily associate with you, such as your name.

PERMISSIONS

Permissions, also known as privileges, control access to the information and equipment on a network. Individual permissions can be set for each file, folder, printer and other equipment on a network. Permissions can deny access or specify the type of access each person on a network receives. For example, an individual may have permission to read a file but not make changes to the file.

WIRELESS NETWORKING

A wireless network allows computers to share information using radio signals instead of cables.

Wireless networks, also known as wi-fi or wireless fidelity networks, are useful when computers are located where cables are not practical. Wireless networks also allow notebook and handheld computers to access a network in any location in an office.

WIRELESS NETWORKING HARDWARE

Desktop Computers

Desktop computers do not usually come with wireless networking hardware. To add wireless networking hardware, you can add a wireless network card, which is an expansion card placed inside a computer. You can also connect a wireless network adapter to a computer through a Universal Serial Bus (USB) connection.

Portable Computers

Many notebook computers and Personal Digital Assistants (PDAs) have built-in wireless networking hardware. To add wireless networking hardware to a notebook computer, you can insert a wireless network PC Card into a computer or connect a wireless network adapter to a computer through a Universal Serial Bus (USB) connection.

Wireless Router

A wireless network requires a wireless router, which is a device that uses radio signals to transfer data between computers on a network. Wireless routers can also allow computers on a wireless network to share one high-speed Internet connection, such as a cable modem or Digital Subscriber Line (DSL). Some wireless routers also allow you to directly connect a printer that all computers on a wireless network can use.

WIRELESS NETWORKING STANDARDS

There are three wireless networking standards used for wireless networks. The two most common standards are 802.11b and 802.11g. Hardware devices used on a network can use one, two or all three standards.

Standard	Speed	Radio Frequency	Compatibility
802.11a	54 Mbps	5 GHz	Cannot work with 802.11b or 802.11g
802.11b	11 Mbps	2.4 GHz	Can work with 802.11g
802.11g	54 Mbps	2.4 GHz	Can work with 802.11b

Mbps stands for megabits per second. GHz stands for gigahertz.

Cost
The 802.11a standard is the most expensive standard, while the 802.11b standard is the least expensive standard.

Interference
The 802.11b standard and the newest 802.11g standard are susceptible to interference from other devices that use the same frequency, such as microwave ovens and cordless phones.

High-Speed 802.11g
Some manufacturers offer a high-speed version of 802.11g, which is not an official wireless networking standard, but offers a speed of up to 108 Mbps. This high-speed version of 802.11g is more expensive and may have more interference problems.

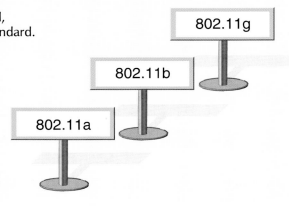

WIRELESS NETWORKING SECURITY

Compared to wired networks, wireless networks are much easier for unauthorized people to access. To help protect data transmitted on a wireless network, there are two security standards that specify the way that data is encrypted, or scrambled, when transmitted over a network—Wired Equivalent Privacy (WEP) and Wireless Protected Access (WPA). WPA offers much more security than WEP.

THE INTERNET AND THE WORLD WIDE WEB

Are you wondering how you can get connected to the Internet and take advantage of all the resources the Web has to offer? This chapter will help you get started.

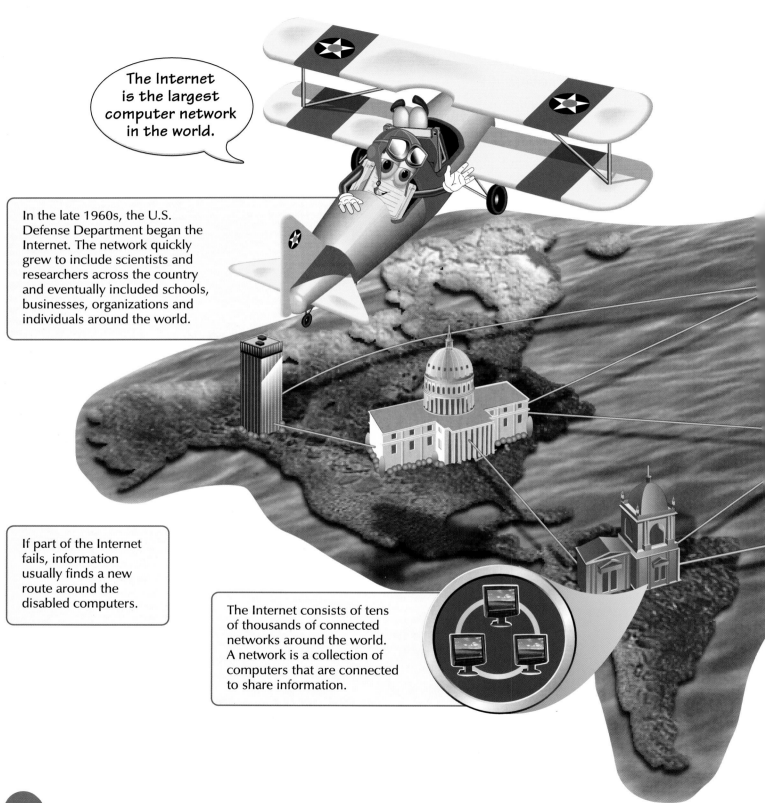

The Internet is the largest computer network in the world.

In the late 1960s, the U.S. Defense Department began the Internet. The network quickly grew to include scientists and researchers across the country and eventually included schools, businesses, organizations and individuals around the world.

If part of the Internet fails, information usually finds a new route around the disabled computers.

The Internet consists of tens of thousands of connected networks around the world. A network is a collection of computers that are connected to share information.

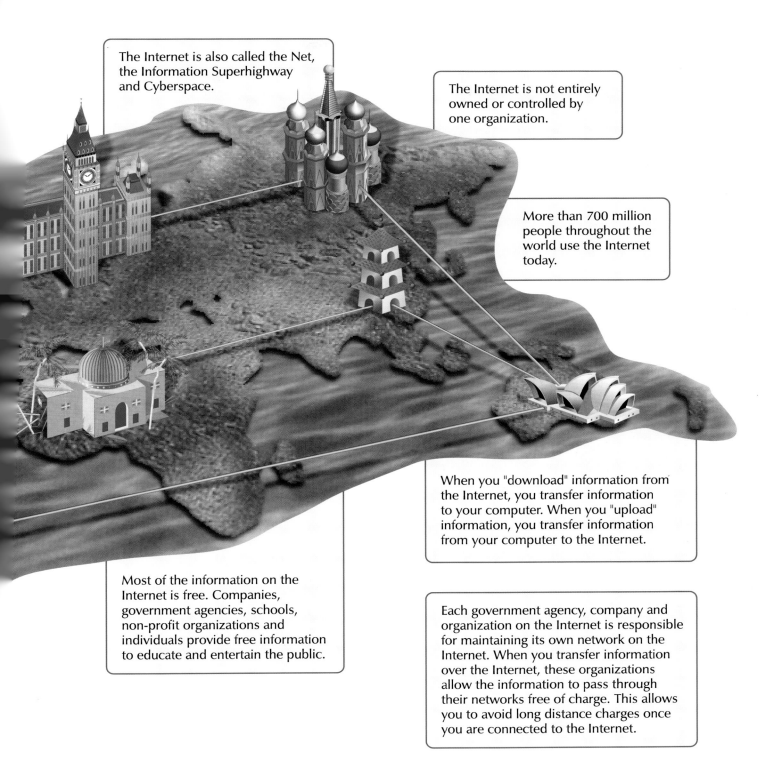

The Internet is also called the Net, the Information Superhighway and Cyberspace.

The Internet is not entirely owned or controlled by one organization.

More than 700 million people throughout the world use the Internet today.

When you "download" information from the Internet, you transfer information to your computer. When you "upload" information, you transfer information from your computer to the Internet.

Most of the information on the Internet is free. Companies, government agencies, schools, non-profit organizations and individuals provide free information to educate and entertain the public.

Each government agency, company and organization on the Internet is responsible for maintaining its own network on the Internet. When you transfer information over the Internet, these organizations allow the information to pass through their networks free of charge. This allows you to avoid long distance charges once you are connected to the Internet.

E-MAIL

Electronic mail, known as e-mail, is the most popular feature on the Internet. You can exchange e-mail with people around the world, including friends, colleagues, family members, customers and even people you meet on the Internet. E-mail is fast, easy, inexpensive and saves paper.

INFORMATION

The Internet provides access to information on any subject imaginable, which makes the Internet a valuable research tool. You can review newspapers, magazines, academic papers, dictionaries, encyclopedias, travel guides, government documents, television show transcripts, recipes, job listings, airline schedules and much more. Many companies, such as the Wall Street Journal, offer premium information, which you can pay a monthly or yearly fee to access.

ENTERTAINMENT

The Internet offers many different forms of entertainment, such as live radio broadcasts, video clips and music. You can find pictures from the latest films, watch interviews with celebrities and listen to your favorite songs. You can also play interactive games with other people around the world.

ONLINE BANKING

Most banks allow you to perform common banking tasks on the Internet. You can pay bills, check your account balances and transfer money between accounts in the comfort of your own home. Online banking offers a fast, easy and convenient way to perform banking tasks and can be done at any time from any location.

ONLINE SHOPPING

You can order goods and services on the Internet without leaving your desk. You can purchase items such as books, flowers, music CDs, DVD movies, toys, pizza, stocks and cars. You can also find programs to use on your computer, including word processors, drawing programs and games. Some companies offer trial versions of programs that you can try for free before deciding if you want to purchase the program.

MESSAGE BOARDS

Message boards on the Internet allow people around the world to read and post messages on topics of interest. You can ask questions, discuss issues and read interesting stories. There are thousands of message boards on topics including computers, health issues, politics and sports. Message boards are also known as bulletin boards.

CHAT

You can exchange typed messages with another person on the Internet. A message you send will instantly appear on the other person's computer. You can chat with one person at a time or with a group of people. You can also join chat rooms where people from around the world can meet and communicate with each other.

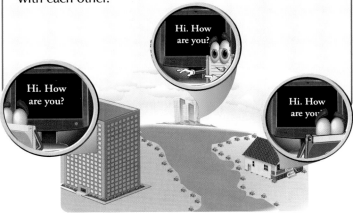

TALK

You can place a long distance telephone call for free or for a substantial discount over the Internet. You use a headset or a microphone and speakers connected to your computer to communicate with the other person. When talking over the Internet, the sound quality can be better than when using telephone lines.

Connecting to
Shawn Lavery
in London, England

GETTING CONNECTED

You can easily connect to the Internet to access all the information the Internet offers.

TYPES OF CONNECTIONS

Modem

Most new computers come with an internal modem, which allows you to connect to the Internet over telephone lines. Connecting to the Internet with a modem is the slowest type of connection, but you can use this type of connection anywhere a telephone line is available.

Cable Modem

A cable modem allows you to connect to the Internet with the same type of cable that attaches to a television set. Compared to a modem connection, a cable modem connection is up to 100 times faster for receiving information and up to 20 times faster for sending information. You can contact your local cable company to determine if they offer cable Internet service.

Cable Modem

DSL

A Digital Subscriber Line (DSL) allows you to connect to the Internet using a high-speed digital phone line. DSL offers the same speeds for sending and receiving information as a cable modem. You can contact your local telephone company to determine if they offer DSL Internet service.

DSL Modem

Satellite

If you cannot obtain a cable modem connection or DSL connection in your area and you want high-speed access to the Internet, you can get satellite Internet access. Compared to a modem connection, a satellite connection is about 10 times faster for receiving information and offers about the same speed for sending information. Satellite Internet access is significantly more expensive than other types of connections.

ADVANTAGES OF HIGH-SPEED CONNECTIONS

High-speed connections include cable modem, DSL and satellite connections. High-speed connections are also known as broadband connections.

Faster

A high-speed Internet connection allows you to access information on the Internet up to 100 times faster than a modem connection. Web pages appear more quickly on your screen, video appears smoother and larger, sound quality is better and files are transferred between computers faster.

Frees Up Telephone Line

Unlike a modem connection, a high-speed Internet connection does not tie up your telephone line while you are connected to the Internet. When you use a high-speed connection, you can make telephone calls or use a fax machine.

24-Hour Connection

A high-speed connection allows you to be connected to the Internet 24 hours a day, which gives you constant access to the Internet. Unlike a modem connection, you do not have to wait for your modem to establish a connection and you will not get any busy signals. You will also not be automatically disconnected if you do not use the connection for a certain period of time.

DISADVANTAGES

A high-speed Internet connection is significantly more expensive than a modem connection. Also, since you can be connected to the Internet 24 hours a day, unauthorized individuals could more easily access your computer. You can obtain firewall software that can help protect your computer from unauthorized access. The latest version of Windows comes with firewall software. Your computer is also safe when your cable modem or DSL modem is turned off.

CHOOSE AN INTERNET SERVICE PROVIDER

An Internet Service Provider (ISP) is a company that gives you access to the Internet for a fee. There are several things you should consider before choosing an ISP.

Cost

Most ISPs offer unlimited access to the Internet for a set fee. Some ISPs offer a certain number of hours or amount of data you can transfer per month for a set fee. If you exceed the total, you may be charged extra.

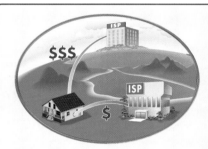

Customer Support

Consider the type of help offered if you run into problems with your Internet connection.

Long Distance Charges

If you are connecting to the Internet with a modem, make sure you choose an ISP with a local telephone number to avoid long distance charges.

Connections
☑ modem
☑ cable modem
☑ DSL

Type of Connection

Make sure the ISP offers the type of connection you want to use to access the Internet, such as modem, cable modem or DSL.

Extra Features

Some ISPs offer additional features, such as parental controls to protect your children from inappropriate content, software to stop unwanted e-mail and the ability to publish your personal Web pages.

References

Before choosing an ISP, ask friends, relatives and colleagues in your area which ISP they use and if they are happy with the service.

COMMERCIAL ONLINE SERVICE

A commercial online service is a type of ISP that offers an enormous amount of well-organized information and services, such as daily news, weather reports and instant messaging. Commercial online services are very easy to use and are ideal for beginners. America Online (AOL) is the most popular commercial online service.

SHARE AN INTERNET CONNECTION

You can set up two or more computers to share a single Internet connection by using a router. A router acts like a traffic cop by managing the flow of information for one Internet connection. Most routers have added security features to help protect the computers from unauthorized access. Each computer sharing the Internet connection must have a Network Interface Card (NIC).

If you want to set up just two computers to share an Internet connection, you can use the Internet Connection Sharing (ICS) software offered in the latest versions of Windows. This software eliminates the need for a router.

WIRELESS INTERNET CONNECTIONS

At Home

You can connect a computer wirelessly to the Internet, which can allow you to use the computer to connect to the Internet in any location in a house, such as in the basement, bedroom or on the deck. Your computer will need a wireless network card, also known as a wi-fi card. You will also need to connect a wireless router to the DSL or cable modem.

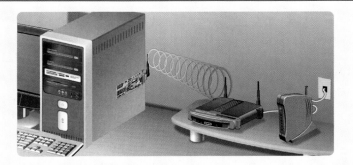

When Traveling

Increasing numbers of public places, such as coffee shops, hotels, airports, trains, airplanes, shopping malls and conference centers, are allowing people to connect to the Internet through wireless networks set up on their premises. These locations are called wi-fi hotspots, or wireless hotspots, and provide a convenient way of accessing the Internet while you are away from home or the office. Your computer will need a wireless network card, also known as a wi-fi card.

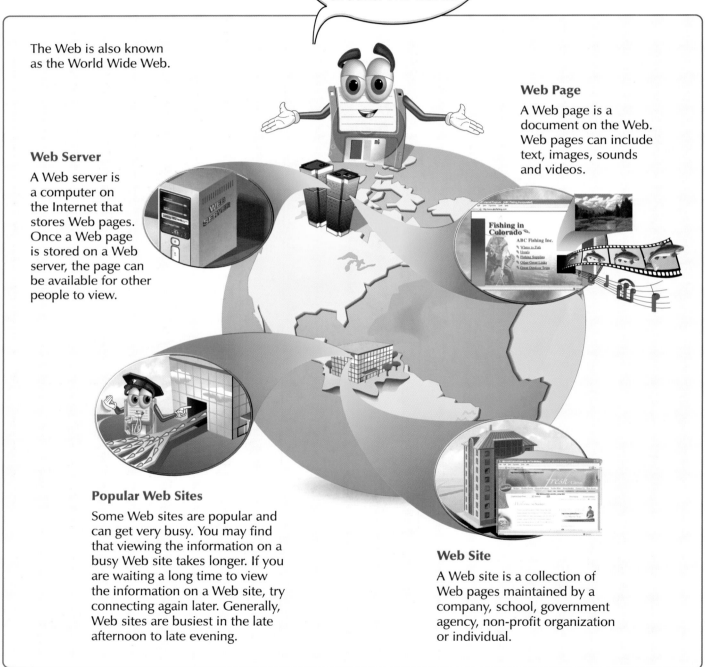

The Web consists of a huge collection of electronic documents stored on computers around the world.

The Web is also known as the World Wide Web.

Web Page

A Web page is a document on the Web. Web pages can include text, images, sounds and videos.

Web Server

A Web server is a computer on the Internet that stores Web pages. Once a Web page is stored on a Web server, the page can be available for other people to view.

Popular Web Sites

Some Web sites are popular and can get very busy. You may find that viewing the information on a busy Web site takes longer. If you are waiting a long time to view the information on a Web site, try connecting again later. Generally, Web sites are busiest in the late afternoon to late evening.

Web Site

A Web site is a collection of Web pages maintained by a company, school, government agency, non-profit organization or individual.

URL

Each Web page has a unique address, called a Uniform Resource Locator (URL). You can instantly display any Web page if you know its URL.

A Web page URL starts with **http** (HyperText Transfer Protocol) and contains the **domain name**, **directory name(s)** and the **name of the Web page**.

When you see or hear about a Web page's URL, the http:// part is usually left out.

The three letters at the end of a domain name can help identify the type of organization or the country that offers the Web site. Here are some common endings.

ORGANIZATION		COUNTRY	
.com	Commercial	.au	Australia
.edu	Educational	.ca	Canada
.gov	Government	.it	Italy
.mil	Military	.jp	Japan
.org	Organization (usually non-profit)	.uk	United Kingdom

LINKS

Web pages contain highlighted text or images, called links or hyperlinks, that connect to other pages on the Web. Links allow you to easily move through a vast amount of information by jumping from one Web page to another, which is known as "browsing the Web." You can select a link to display a Web page located on the same computer or a computer across the city, country or world.

You can easily identify text links on a Web page because they often appear underlined and in color.

WEB BROWSER

POPULAR WEB BROWSERS

Internet Explorer is currently the most popular Web browser. Internet Explorer comes with the Windows operating system. Other available Web browsers include Firefox, Mozilla, Netscape, Opera and Safari.

THE WEB BROWSER SCREEN

Web browsers have a similar look and work in a similar way.

■ This area displays the address of the Web page you are currently viewing. You can instantly display any Web page by typing its address into this area.

■ This area displays a symbol (🔒) when you are viewing a secure Web site. You can safely transfer confidential information, such as a credit card number, to a secure Web site.

■ This area displays a toolbar to help you quickly perform common tasks.

■ This area displays a Web page. When you position your mouse ⟍ over highlighted text or an image and the mouse ⟍ changes to a different symbol, such as ⟍, you can click the text or image to display a linked Web page.

WEB BROWSER FEATURES

Home Page

The home page is the Web page that appears each time you start your Web browser. You can choose any page on the Web as your home page. Make sure you choose a home page that provides a good starting point for exploring the Web.

Navigation Buttons

Web browsers provide buttons to help you move through information on the Web. You can move back and forward through Web pages you have viewed or stop the transfer of a Web page that is taking a long time to appear.

Favorites

Web browsers have a feature, called favorites or bookmarks, which allows you to store the addresses of Web pages you frequently visit. The favorites feature saves you from having to remember and constantly retype your favorite Web page addresses. You can organize the Web pages in your favorites list to help you more quickly find Web pages of interest.

History List

When you are browsing through pages on the Web, keeping track of the pages you have visited can be difficult. Most Web browsers include a history list that allows you to quickly return to any Web page you have recently visited.

MEDIA ON THE WEB

You can view and play many types of media on the Web, including images, sounds and videos.

To be able to view and play most types of media on the Web, make sure you have the latest version of a Web browser installed on your computer. For the latest version of Internet Explorer, which is the most popular Web browser for Windows computers, visit www.microsoft.com.

FILE EXTENSIONS

Some Web pages display the file extensions of file names. A file extension is the three characters that appear after the period in a file name and indicate the type of file. For example, rose.jpg is an image file and baby.mov is a movie file. Knowing the file extension of a file can help you determine whether you can play the file on your computer and, if not, what software you need to play the file.

IMAGES

You can view images on the Web, including photographs, paintings, drawings, maps, charts, diagrams and background images.

Common Types of Images:

• GIF (.gif): Illustrations and computer-generated art
• JPEG (.jpg): Photographs and paintings

Web pages can also display animated GIFs that rotate through a series of images.

SOUNDS

You can listen to sounds on the Web, including songs, famous speeches, sound effects, live radio broadcasts and sound clips from television shows and movies.

Common Types of Sounds:

- MIDI (.mid): Background music
- MP3 (.mp3): Songs
- WAVE (.wav): Short sound clips
- WMA (.wma): Songs
- Real Audio (.ra, .rm, .ram): Live radio station broadcasts If your computer cannot play Real Audio sounds, you can obtain RealPlayer software at www.real.com.

NON-MEDIA FILES

You will also see non-media files on the Web. Be careful when running .exe files on your computer since these files could contain viruses which can damage your computer.

Common Types of Files:

- Executable (.exe): Programs
- Portable Document Format (.pdf): Documents If you cannot view PDF files on your computer, you can obtain Adobe Reader at www.adobe.com.

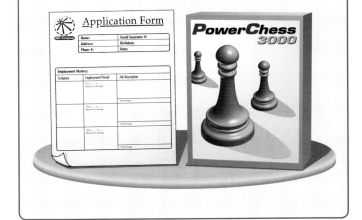

VIDEOS

You can view video on the Web, including Hollywood movie clips, animations, interviews with celebrities, tutorials and eye-catching visual effects.

Common Types of Videos:

- AVI (.avi): Home movies
- Flash (.swf): Animations
- MPEG (.mpg): Home movies
- Quicktime (.mov): Hollywood movie trailers
- Real Video (.rm, .ram): Television broadcasts
- Shockwave (.dcr): Games

If your computer cannot play a video, you can obtain software to play the video at one of the following Web sites:

Flash Player (www.macromedia.com)

QuickTime Player (www.apple.com/quicktime)

RealPlayer (www.real.com)

Shockwave Player (www.macromedia.com)

You can use the many free services available on the Web to find information of interest to you.

SEARCH FOR WEB PAGES

Use a Search Engine

A search engine allows you to search for information on the Web. You can type a word or phrase of interest and a search engine will display a list of Web pages that match the information you specified. You can use popular search engines by visiting the following Web sites:

www.google.com

www.msn.com

www.yahoo.com

How Search Engines Find Web Pages

Search engines use programs, called robots or spiders, to find pages on the Web. People can also submit information about Web pages they have created to search engines. Since thousands of new Web pages are created every day, search engines cannot possibly index every new page on the Web.

The Search Results

When you use a search engine to find pages on the Web, some of the pages may have moved or been removed from the Web. If a Web page has moved or no longer exists, some search engines allow you to display a page as it appeared when the search engine indexed the page—known as a "Cached" Web page.

Search by Category

Most search engines allow you to browse through categories to find Web pages of interest. For example, you can browse through categories such as business, computers, games, health, kids, news, reference, science, shopping and sports. Volunteers often review and categorize each Web page.

SEARCH FOR PEOPLE

Some Web sites allow you to find street addresses, telephone numbers and e-mail addresses for friends, relatives, colleagues and businesses. You can visit the following Web sites to search for people of interest:

people.yahoo.com

www.411.com

www.whitepages.com

Some Web sites offer a paid service that performs a more comprehensive search for people of interest. You can visit the www.intelus.com and www.peopledata.com Web sites to perform a more comprehensive search.

SEARCH FOR MAPS AND DIRECTIONS

Some Web sites allow you to display a map for a street address you enter. You can also obtain driving directions between a starting address and a destination address and may even be able to obtain information about tourist attractions, restaurants and hotels along the way. You can visit the following Web sites for maps and driving directions:

maps.yahoo.com

www.mapquest.com

www.mappoint.com

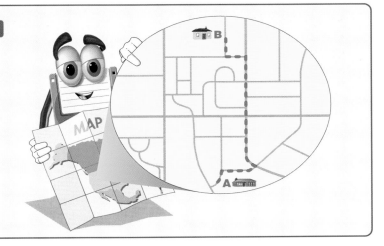

SEARCH FOR IMAGES

Many search engines allow you to search for images such as pictures of your favorite celebrities or paintings. You can type a word or phrase that describes an image of interest and the search engine will display all the images that match the text you typed.

SHOPPING ON THE WEB

You can buy products on the Web without ever leaving your home or office.

The Web offers millions of products that you can purchase, including books, clothing, electronic equipment, toys, DVD movies and computer programs. You can even purchase groceries and items from online gift registries on the Web. Nearly everything you can buy in a store, you can now buy on the Web.

ADVANTAGES OF SHOPPING ON THE WEB

Convenience

Shopping on the Web can be more convenient than shopping in traditional stores. You can shop on the Web twenty-four hours a day, seven days a week. The Web also gives you access to stores around the world, which is useful if you live in a rural area where a wide variety of stores are not available.

Lower Prices

Popular products sold on the Web are generally available at lower prices compared to traditional stores since companies that sell products on the Web often do not have overhead costs, such as rent and salespeople. Most companies charge for delivery, so make sure you consider the delivery charge before ordering a product.

Comparison Shopping

Before you buy a product, you can use the Web to compare products and prices offered by different companies. Two popular Web sites that help you compare products are froogle.google.com and www.mysimon.com. You can also obtain reviews from other customers on the Web to help you make an informed decision before making a purchase. A popular Web site that offers customer reviews is www.epinions.com.

TYPES OF SHOPPING WEB SITES

Companies

Many companies have Web sites where you can purchase their products online. You can also view product pictures, details and pricing information to help you make your purchase. Some Web sites specialize in a certain type of merchandise while other Web sites offer a variety of products from many different companies. Some popular shopping Web sites are:

www.amazon.com
shopping.yahoo.com
www.walmart.com

Auctions

You can find auctions on the Web where you can bid on products such as clothing, consumer electronics, jewelry, toys and much more. Auctions are ideal for obtaining great prices on used items and purchasing unique or difficult to find items, such as collectibles or out-of-print books. The most popular auction Web site is www.ebay.com.

SHOPPING CONSIDERATIONS

Security

Security is important when you want to send confidential information, such as a credit card number, over the Internet. Before sending confidential information to a Web site, make sure the site is secure.

The address of a secure Web site usually starts with **https** rather than **http**. When viewing a secure Web site in Internet Explorer, a lock symbol (🔒) appears at the bottom of your screen, indicating the Web site is secure.

Returns

When ordering a product, you could be ordering from a company located in a different state or country, which can make it more difficult to return a product you do not find suitable. You should check the company's return policy before ordering a product.

There are many ways you can ensure that browsing the Web is a safe and positive experience for your children.

Most of the information on the Web is meant to educate or entertain, but some Web pages may contain material that is inappropriate for children. Web pages can contain pornography or violent, hateful, illegal or dangerous content.

SUPERVISE YOUR CHILDREN

Constant adult supervision is the best way to ensure your children do not access inappropriate information on the Web. Although there are many tools you can obtain to help protect your children, these tools should never replace parental supervision.

Here are some tips:

- Keep the family computer in a high traffic area in your house, such as the kitchen or family room, so you can monitor all online activity.

- Tell your children not to provide their photo or personal details, such as their name, address, phone number or school name.

- Tell your children they are not allowed to meet in person with anyone they have met online.

INTERNET SERVICE PROVIDERS

Many Internet service providers (ISPs) offer parental controls that help protect children while they are online. For example, America Online (AOL) offers parental controls that allow you to monitor your children's online activity. AOL also allows you to decide which Web sites your children can access and who they can communicate with. Check with your ISP to see what features they offer to make your children's Web browsing experience safer.

SEARCH ENGINES FOR KIDS

Many search engines are available that are designed for kids. These search engines are friendly, easy to use and filter out content that is inappropriate for children. You can visit the following Web sites for kid-friendly search engines:

kidsclick.org

www.ajkids.com

yahooligans.yahoo.com

WEB BROWSERS FOR KIDS

You can obtain a Web browser designed for children that allows children to safely explore information on the Web. Web browsers for kids are easy to use, fun and only allow access to Web pages that are appropriate for children. You can visit the following Web sites to obtain kid-friendly Web browsers:

www.devicode.com/kidsplorer

www.kidrocket.org

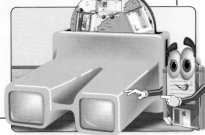

CHAT ROOMS FOR KIDS

Many kid-friendly Web sites provide chat rooms where children can instantly communicate with other kids from around the world by exchanging typed messages. Adults monitor the chats to keep the chats safe and fun. The following are some Web sites that offer chats monitored by adults:

www.headbonezone.com

www.kidscom.com

www.kidzworld.com

PARENTAL CONTROL SOFTWARE

You can purchase software that helps you control your children's experience on the Internet. Some of the most commonly offered features of parental control software are:

- Blocking unsuitable Web sites.

- Blocking or controlling access to online activities, such as chat rooms, e-mail and instant messaging.

- Preventing children from giving out their personal information.

- Preventing children from going online at times you specify, such as when you are away at work.

You can visit the following Web sites to obtain parental control software:

www.cyberpatrol.com

www.filterlogixathome.com

www.netnanny.com

CREATE AND PUBLISH WEB PAGES

You can create and publish Web pages to share information with people around the world.

Individuals publish Web pages to share their favorite pictures, hobbies and interests. Companies publish Web pages to promote their businesses, advertise products, publicize job openings and provide contact information.

CREATE WEB PAGES

Most people use a Web site creation program, such as Microsoft FrontPage, to create Web pages. These programs help you visually create Web pages and organize all the pages in your Web site.

You can also create Web pages in the following ways:

- Many programs, such as Microsoft Word and QuarkXPress, allow you to save documents you create as Web pages.

- You can create Web pages by typing the code used to create Web pages—HTML—into a document. HTML is often used by programmers to create Web pages.

- Some Web sites, such as www.site2you.com and www.handzon.com, allow you to create Web pages quickly and easily online for a fee. These Web sites provide pre-designed templates you can choose from that take you through the process of creating your Web pages.

REGISTER YOUR OWN DOMAIN NAME

A domain name is the address that people type to access your Web pages, such as www.maran.com. A personalized domain name is easy for people to remember. If you obtain a personalized domain name, make sure the domain name is registered in your name so if you later choose a different company to publish your Web pages, you can take the name with you. For information on registering your own domain name, visit the www.internic.net Web site.

WEB PAGE CONTENT CONSIDERATIONS

Before you start creating Web pages, examine some of your favorite Web pages to get ideas.

• You should change your Web pages on a regular basis to keep the pages interesting and up-to-date so people will return to your pages.

• When creating your Web pages, try to keep the file size of the pages and images as small as possible to speed up the display of your pages.

• Always include contact information on Web pages you create to allow readers to contact you if they have questions or comments.

PUBLISH WEB PAGES

When you finish creating your Web pages, you can transfer the pages to a company that will make them available on the Web. You can choose from several types of companies to publish your Web pages.

Internet Service Providers

Internet Service Providers (ISPs), which are companies that offer people access to the Internet, often allow their customers to publish Web pages for free or for a fee. ISPs provide the easiest and most convenient way to publish Web pages.

Web Hosting Service Providers

Web hosting service providers, also known as Web presence providers, specialize in publishing Web pages. These companies charge a fee, but provide the most flexibility and features for publishing Web pages. You can visit the www.hosting.com, www.verio.com and www.webhosting.com Web sites to publish your pages.

Free Web Page Publishing

Some companies on the Web will publish your Web pages for free. These companies usually display advertisements when people view your pages. You can visit the www.fortunecity.com, www.freeservers.com and www.netfirms.com Web sites to publish your Web pages for free.

A blog typically documents the day-to-day life of an individual. You can find millions of blogs covering every topic from art and music to news, politics, technology and more.

A blog, short for Web log, is a personal journal or diary that is available on the Web.

WHO CREATES BLOGS?

Most people create blogs to discuss their personal experiences, hobbies and family events. A blog provides a great way to keep in touch with family members and friends. Blogs are also created by professional and amateur journalists to publish breaking news, as well as by companies to discuss company-related information.

Most blogs are created by individuals, but you can also find group blogs on the Web. A group blog provides a great way for a family, group of friends, club, team or a school class to share news and information. With a group blog, all members of the blog can add entries to the blog.

FIND BLOGS

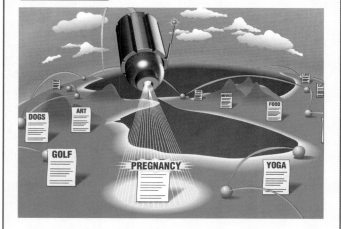

You can use blog directories to search for blogs that share your interests. Blog directories allow you to search for specific blogs by entering a topic of interest or by browsing through categories. Two popular blog directories include Daypop (www.daypop.com) and Blog Search Engine (www.blogsearchengine.com).

You can also use a search engine such as Google (www.google.com) or Yahoo! (www.yahoo.com) to search for blogs of interest. For example, to find a blog about pregnancy, search for "pregnancy blog."

CREATE A BLOG

Blogs are very popular because people with little or no technical knowledge can update and maintain a blog. In most cases, to create a blog, you will answer a few simple questions using an online form and within minutes your blog will be available on the Web.

You can find many blog hosting services on the Web, which help you create and store a blog. The Blogger Web site (www.blogger.com) is a popular Web site that allows you to create a blog for free.

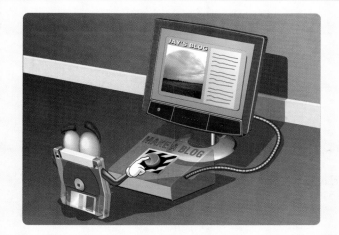

BLOG CONTENT

When you want to add a new entry to a blog, you simply type a message and click a button. Almost immediately, the entry will appear in the blog. People typically update a blog every day to keep visitors coming back.

You can add photos to a blog as well as links to relevant sources of information. Some blog hosting services

allow you to call the service from a telephone and leave a message that is immediately posted to the blog as a sound file.

When visitors read your blog, they can comment on what you share in your blog. Visitor comments will appear on the blog for everyone to read.

PUBLICIZE A BLOG

After you create a blog, you need to publicize the blog so people can find and add comments to the blog. At first, you should tell your friends, family members and colleagues about the blog. Every time you send an e-mail message, you can add a link to the blog at the end of the message. You can also trade links with other bloggers. Ask another blogger if they will include a link to your blog if you will do the same.

MESSAGE BOARDS

A message board is a discussion group that allows people with common interests to communicate with each other.

There are thousands of message boards on every subject imaginable. Each message board discusses a particular topic, such as parenting, diets, sports or regional issues.

Message boards provided on Web sites are easy to use and do not require you to install any special software on your computer. You view messages using your Web browser.

WHERE TO FIND A MESSAGE BOARD

You can look for message boards on your favorite Web sites. Some Web sites offer message boards that are dedicated to the subject of the Web site. For example, a Web site devoted to playing the guitar may offer a message board where you can communicate with other people about playing the guitar.

You can also visit Web sites that offer a wide range of message boards for you to choose from, such as messages.yahoo.com and www.ezboard.com. You can type in a topic of interest to find related boards and messages or browse through categories for a message board of interest.

HOW MESSAGE BOARDS WORK

Sending a message to a message board is similar to tacking a notice on a public bulletin board. You leave your message on the board so other people can read the message and respond to it at a later time. Your message is usually posted on the board within a few seconds, but it might take a while for other people to send a response.

MESSAGE BOARD TIPS

Protect Your Privacy

Many Web sites require you to create a profile before you can post and respond to messages on a message board. When creating a profile, you may want to consider using a nickname to keep your identity private. You should also avoid including any personal contact information in messages you post to a message board.

Post a Message

You can send, or post, a new message to a message board to ask a question or express an opinion. Thousands of people around the world may read a message you post. Each message board has its own rules and style, so make sure you read any available introductory information before posting to a message board.

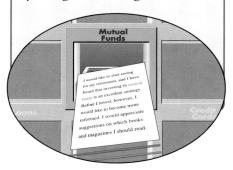

Moderators

Some message boards have moderators to monitor the messages posted to the board. A moderator is a person who reviews each message that is posted to a message board to ensure the message is appropriate and on topic. For example, if someone posts an advertisement to the board, the moderator may remove it from the board.

GOOGLE GROUPS

You can use Google Groups (groups.google.com) to view messages in Usenet newsgroups. Usenet newsgroups were the original Internet version of message boards. Google Groups allows you to browse through messages and search for information in the more than 650 million Usenet newsgroup messages. You can also post messages to Usenet newsgroups through Google Groups, but you must first sign up for a Google account.

WEB-BASED CHAT

You can communicate with people around the world by exchanging typed messages, which is called chatting.

Chatting is a feature offered by many Web sites. When chatting, the message you send immediately appears on the screen of every person in the conversation.

CHAT ROOMS

A chat room is an area of a Web site where people can go to chat. Each chat room is usually devoted to a particular topic, such as yoga, dog training or playing piano. Some Web sites, such as www.talkcity.com, offer a wide range of chat rooms for you to choose from. Other Web sites may only offer one or two chat rooms that are dedicated to the subject of the Web site. For example, a Web site devoted to knitting may offer a chat room that focuses on knitting-related topics.

WEB BROWSER

You can use your Web browser to visit a chat room. Most Web-based chat rooms do not require you to install any additional software on your computer. To ensure you can access most Web-based chat rooms, make sure you have the latest version of your Web browser installed on your computer.

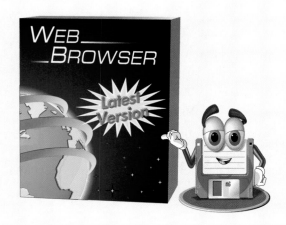

CHATTING TIPS

Nickname

When you visit a chat room, you have to sign in and give yourself a nickname. Using a nickname instead of your real name helps protect your privacy.

Lurking

Lurking is a good way to get the feel of a chat room and find out if it is a place you want to join in on a conversation. When you enter a new chat room, watch the conversation for a few minutes. If you like the way the conversation is going, join in. If you do not like the way the conversation is going, just leave and find a different chat room that is more suitable.

Firewalls

If your company or Internet service provider has set up a firewall to protect your computer from unauthorized access, you may have problems accessing chat rooms that use Java. Java is a programming language used to display the text in many Web-based chat rooms. You should contact your network administrator or service provider if you are having problems accessing chat rooms that use Java.

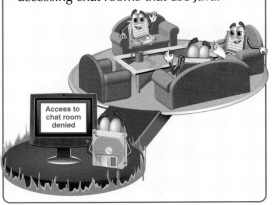

Abbreviations

In chat rooms, participants in a conversation often use abbreviations of long words and phrases to save time typing and help the conversation flow faster.

Private Chats

Instead of chatting with all the people in a chat room, you can have a private conversation with just one other chat room participant. Having a private conversation in a chat room is sometimes called whispering.

CHAPTER 11

E-MAIL AND INSTANT MESSAGING

Are you ready to communicate with other people on the Internet? This chapter introduces you to e-mail and instant messages.

You can exchange electronic mail (e-mail) with people around the world.

E-mail is a fast, economical and convenient way to send messages to family, friends and colleagues.

E-MAIL PROGRAMS

An e-mail program lets you send, receive and manage your e-mail messages.

Popular e-mail programs include Microsoft's Outlook and Outlook Express, IBM's Lotus Notes and Qualcomm's Eudora.

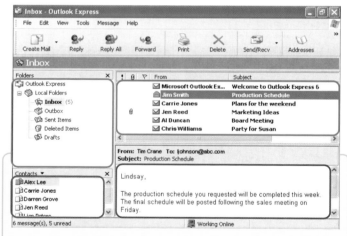

Outlook Express

■ This area displays the folders that contain your e-mail messages.

■ This area displays a list of all your e-mail messages.

■ This area displays the contents of a single e-mail message.

■ This area displays a list of your contacts.

You can send a message to anyone around the world if you know the person's e-mail address.

mvickers@sales.abc.com

An e-mail address defines the location of an individual's mailbox on the Internet.

PARTS OF AN E-MAIL ADDRESS

An e-mail address consists of two parts separated by the @ ("at") symbol. An e-mail address cannot contain spaces.

mvickers@sales.abc.com

■ The **user name** is the name of the person's account. This can be a real name or a nickname. The user name should also be easy for other people to remember and spell.

■ The **domain name** is the location of the person's account on the Internet. Periods (.) separate the various parts of the domain name.

ORGANIZATION OR COUNTRY

The last few characters in an e-mail address usually indicate the type of organization the person belongs to or the country the person lives in.

ORGANIZATION		COUNTRY	
.com	commercial	.au	Australia
.edu	education	.ca	Canada
.gov	government	.fr	France
.mil	military	.it	Italy
.net	network	.jp	Japan
.org	organization (often non-profit)	.uk	United Kingdom

You can send an e-mail message to exchange ideas or request information.

When you send a message, do not assume the person will read the message right away. Some people may not regularly check their messages.

If you want to test your e-mail or practice sending a message, send a message to yourself.

COST

E-mail is a cost-effective way to communicate with other people. Once you pay a service provider for a connection to the Internet, there is no charge for sending and receiving e-mail. You do not have to pay extra even if you send a long message, send attached files or send the message around the world.

Exchanging e-mail can save you money on long distance calls. The next time you are about to pick up the telephone, consider sending an e-mail message instead.

CONVENIENCE

Sending information by e-mail is often more convenient than other forms of communication. You can attach files, such as documents or images, to your messages and send them instantly instead of waiting for the files to be sent by regular mail or courier.

E-mail also allows you to quickly and easily send information to many people at once. For example, you can send an announcement about an upcoming sale to all of your customers at the same time.

MESSAGE TIPS

Writing Style

Make sure every message you send is clear, concise and contains no spelling or grammar errors. Also make sure the message will not be misinterpreted. For example, the reader may not realize a statement is meant to be sarcastic.

A MESSAGE WRITTEN IN CAPITAL LETTERS, CALLED SHOUTING, IS ANNOYING AND HARD TO READ. Always use a combination of uppercase and lowercase letters when typing messages.

Smileys

You can use special characters, called smileys or emoticons, to express emotions in messages. These characters resemble human faces if you turn them sideways.

SMILEYS

Gesture	Characters
Cry	:'-(
Frown	:-(
Indifferent	:-I
Laugh	:-D
Smile	:-)
Surprise	:-O
Wink	;-)

Format Text

Most e-mail programs allow you to add formatting to the text in your e-mail messages. For example, you can change the font, size and color of text in a message to make the text easier to read or draw attention to important information.

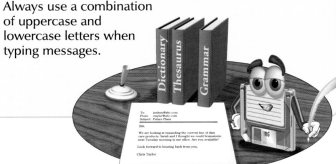

Signature

You can have an e-mail program add information about yourself to the end of every message you send. This prevents you from having to repeatedly type the same information. A signature can include your name, occupation, e-mail address or favorite quotation.

WORK WITH MESSAGES

There are many ways you can work with e-mail messages.

RECEIVE A MESSAGE

Your computer does not have to be turned on to receive an e-mail message. Your Internet service provider stores the messages you receive in a mailbox. When you check for new messages, you are checking your mailbox on the service provider's computer. Make sure you regularly check for messages.

You can use most computers on the Internet to connect to your service provider and retrieve messages. This allows you to check your messages when traveling.

FORWARD A MESSAGE

After reading a message you receive, you can add comments and then send the message to a friend or colleague.

AUTOMATICALLY CHECK FOR MESSAGES

Most e-mail programs automatically check for new e-mail messages for you. You can specify how often you want the program to check for new messages. You may want to have your e-mail program check for messages every 30 minutes.

FIND A MESSAGE

If you cannot find a message you want to review, most e-mail programs allow you to search for the message. For example, you can search for a message you received from a specific person or a message that contains specific text.

REPLY TO A MESSAGE

You can reply to a message you receive to answer a question, express an opinion or supply additional information.

MESSAGES

REPLIES

Quoting

When you reply to a message, make sure you include part of the original message. This is called quoting. Quoting helps the reader identify which message you are replying to.

To save the reader time, make sure you delete all parts of the original message that do not relate to your reply.

REVIEW AN ATTACHED FILE

An e-mail message you receive may include an attached file that you can open and view on your computer. If the attached file contains a virus, the virus can spread to your computer when you open the file. You should only open an attached file sent by a person you trust.

A virus is a program that disrupts the normal operation of a computer and can cause a variety of computer problems. You should use a virus scanner to check e-mail messages for viruses. You can find popular virus scanners at the www.mcafee.com and www.symantec.com Web sites.

ATTACH A FILE TO A MESSAGE

You can attach a document, image, sound or video to a message you are sending. The computer receiving the message must have a program that can display or play the file.

You should try to keep the size of an attached file under 10 MB, since many companies that provide e-mail accounts do not allow you to send messages with large attached files.

If you want to share a file that is over 10 MB, you can send the file on a recordable disc by regular mail or courier instead.

MAKE E-MAIL MORE EFFICIENT

> Most e-mail programs include several features that help you send and receive messages more efficiently.

ADDRESS BOOK

Most e-mail programs provide an address book where you can store the e-mail addresses of people you frequently send messages to. An address book saves you from having to type the same e-mail addresses over and over again.

You can also create groups within your address book to allow you to send a message to many e-mail addresses at once. For example, you can create a group that contains the e-mail addresses of all of your colleagues or a group that contains the e-mail addresses of all of your clients. When you send a message to the group, the message will be sent to every e-mail address in the group.

AUTOMATIC REPLIES

Most e-mail programs have a feature that allows your computer to send automatic replies to e-mail messages you receive, even when you are not at your computer. Sending automatic replies is useful if you are going on vacation. For example, each person who sends you a message while you are away could receive a reply indicating when you will return. To send automatic replies, your computer must be turned on and connected to the Internet.

SORT INCOMING MESSAGES

You can have an e-mail program sort the messages you receive. Sorting incoming messages allows the e-mail program to organize incoming messages before you read them. For example, you could have the program sort all the messages you receive from your friends into a Personal folder so the messages are easy for you to locate.

There are several Web sites that allow you to send and receive e-mail on the Web free of charge.

You use your Web browser to send and receive Web-based e-mail. You do not need an e-mail program installed on your computer.

You can find popular Web-based e-mail services at the following Web sites:
www.hotmail.com
www.gmail.com
mail.yahoo.com

WORLDWIDE ACCESS

When you use a Web-based e-mail service, you can access your e-mail from any computer in the world that has access to the Web. Web-based e-mail is useful for people who need to access their e-mail while traveling.

PERMANENT E-MAIL ADDRESS

Using a Web-based e-mail service allows you to obtain an e-mail address that will not change. This lets you keep the same e-mail address even if you switch to a new Internet service provider.

MESSAGE STORAGE SPACE

When choosing a Web-based e-mail service, make sure you choose a service that offers adequate storage space for the e-mail messages you send and receive. If your Web-based mailbox gets too full, the e-mail service provider may delete some of your messages.

REDUCING SPAM

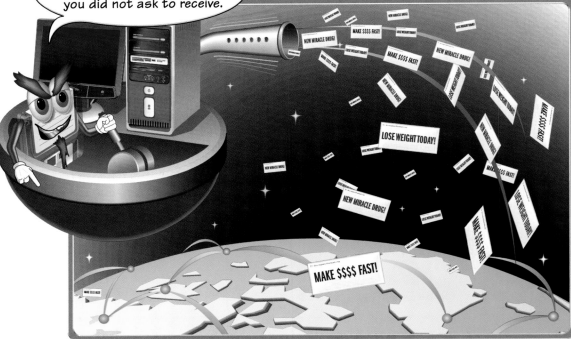

Spam refers to any unwanted e-mail message that you did not ask to receive.

Spam messages may include advertisements, chain letters, fake virus warnings or petitions and are usually sent to a large number of people at once.

REDUCE THE AMOUNT OF SPAM YOU RECEIVE

There are many ways you can reduce the amount of spam you receive.

Use Multiple E-mail Addresses

Keep a primary e-mail address for exchanging messages with your friends, family and colleagues and use a secondary e-mail address for participating in message boards or chats, joining online contests or purchasing products online. This way, if your e-mail address is added to a spammer's list, all the spam will go to the secondary e-mail address instead of your primary e-mail address. You can set up a free, Web-based e-mail address from a service such as Hotmail (www.hotmail.com).

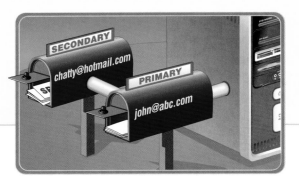

Do Not Click "Remove Me"

Do not click the "Remove Me" link that appears at the bottom of many spam messages. Your e-mail address will often not be removed from the spammer's list and may actually be added to even more lists. Similarly, do not sign up for a service on the Internet that claims to remove your e-mail address from spammers' lists.

REDUCE THE AMOUNT OF SPAM YOU RECEIVE (Continued)

Do Not Buy From Spammers

The best way to stop spammers from sending advertisements is for people not to buy their advertised products. If you purchase products advertised by spam, you prove to the spammers that their advertising methods work and encourage them to send even more spam.

USE SPAM FILTERING PROGRAMS

Spam Filtering Programs

There are many spam filtering programs that you can use to reduce the amount of spam you receive. McAfee's SpamKiller and GIANT Company's Spam Inspector are two popular programs.

You can also use a community-based spam filter on the Internet, such as Cloudmark's SpamNet. Every member of a spam filter community works together to reduce the amount of spam sent to other members.

How Spam Filtering Programs Work

Spam filtering programs may use one or more methods to block spam messages. The programs may automatically block messages from certain addresses, only allow delivery of messages from addresses you have specified as "safe," or block messages containing specific text, such as "make money fast." Keep in mind that spam filtering programs are not perfect. Valid e-mail messages may be mistakenly blocked by a program. Most spam filtering programs place blocked messages in a Spam or Junk folder, so you can review the blocked messages.

INSTANT MESSAGING

INSTANT MESSAGING PROGRAM

You need to install an instant messaging program on your computer to exchange instant messages with other people. You and the people you want to exchange messages with must use compatible instant messaging programs. You can find popular instant messaging programs at the following Web sites:

AOL Instant Messenger
www.aim.com

MSN Messenger
messenger.msn.com

Yahoo! Messenger
messenger.yahoo.com

Contact List

Instant messaging programs provide a contact list where you can save the identities of people you frequently exchange messages with. After you add a person to your contact list, your instant messaging program will notify you when the person goes online.

REASONS FOR INSTANT MESSAGES

Communicate

Sending instant messages is ideal for communicating with people who are located around the world. Once you see that one of your contacts is online, you can immediately start typing to communicate with them.

Meet New People

You can meet people on the Internet who use an instant messaging program. When people register with an instant messaging program, they can enter information about themselves, such as their occupation, hobbies and interests. You may be able to use this information to find and communicate with people who share your interests.

COMMUNICATE USING INSTANT MESSAGES

Abbreviations

To save time when exchanging instant messages, many people type abbreviations for commonly used words and phrases. For example, you could type "cu l8r" instead of "see you later" or type "brb" instead of "be right back."

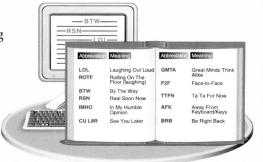

Voice and Video Conversations

Many instant messaging programs allow you to have voice conversations and communicate with your contacts through live video. You need a microphone and speakers to participate in a voice conversation, as well as a webcam, which is a small device used to transmit video, to participate in a video conversation. Since sound and video transfer over the Internet more slowly than text, you should have a high-speed connection to the Internet to participate in voice and video conversations.

Cell Phones and Mobile Devices

Most instant messaging programs allow you to send instant messages to cell phones that have text messaging capabilities and other mobile devices, such as PDAs (Personal Digital Assistants). This allows you to keep in touch with your contacts even when they are away from their computer.

INDEX

INDEX

GUITAR

MARAN ILLUSTRATED™ Guitar is an excellent resource for people who want to learn to play the guitar, as well as for current musicians who want to fine tune their technique. This full-color guide includes over 500 photographs, accompanied by step-by-step instructions that teach you the basics of playing the guitar and reading music, as well as advanced guitar techniques. You will also learn what to look for when purchasing a guitar or accessories, how to maintain and repair your guitar and much more.

Whether you want to learn to strum your favorite tunes or play professionally, MARAN ILLUSTRATED™ Guitar provides all the information you need to become a proficient guitarist.

BOOK BONUS!

Visit **www.maran.com/guitar** to download MP3 files you can listen to and play along with for all the chords, scales, exercises and practice pieces in the book.

ISBN: 1-59200-860-7
Price: $24.99 US; $33.95 CDN
Page count: 320

PIANO

MARAN ILLUSTRATED™ Piano is an information-packed resource for people who want to learn to play the piano, as well as current musicians looking to hone their skills. Combining full-color photographs and easy-to-follow instructions, this guide covers everything from the basics of piano playing to more advanced techniques. Not only does MARAN ILLUSTRATED™ Piano show you how to read music, play scales and chords and improvise while playing with other musicians, it also provides you with helpful information for purchasing and caring for your piano. You will also learn what to look for when you buy a piano or piano accessories, how to find the best location for your piano and how to clean your piano.

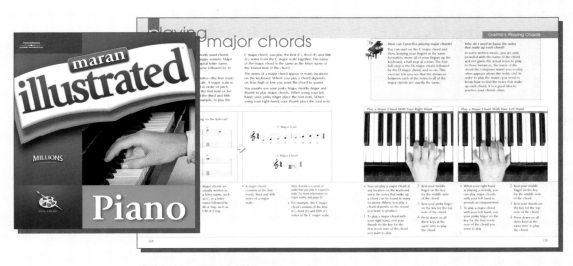

ISBN: 1-59200-864-X
Price: $24.99 US; $33.95 CDN
Page count: 304

DOG TRAINING

MARAN ILLUSTRATED™ Dog Training is an excellent guide for both current dog owners and people considering making a dog part of their family. Using clear, step-by-step instructions accompanied by over 400 full-color photographs, MARAN ILLUSTRATED™ Dog Training is perfect for any visual learner who prefers seeing what to do rather than reading lengthy explanations.

Beginning with insights into popular dog breeds and puppy development, this book emphasizes positive training methods to guide you through socializing, housetraining and teaching your dog many commands. You will also learn how to work with problem behaviors, such as destructive chewing, excessive barking and separation anxiety.

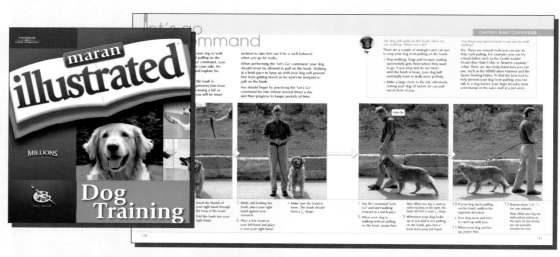

ISBN: 1-59200-858-5
Price: $19.99 US; $26.95 CDN
Page count: 256

KNITTING & CROCHETING

MARAN ILLUSTRATED™ Knitting & Crocheting contains a wealth of information about these two increasingly popular crafts. Whether you are just starting out or you are an experienced knitter or crocheter interested in picking up new tips and techniques, this information-packed resource will take you from the basics, such as how to hold the knitting needles or crochet hook and create different types of stitches, to more advanced skills, such as how to add decorative touches to your projects and fix mistakes. The easy-to-follow information is communicated through clear, step-by-step instructions and accompanied by over 600 full-color photographs—perfect for any visual learner.

This book also includes numerous easy-to-follow patterns for all kinds of items, from simple crocheted scarves to cozy knitted baby outfits.

ISBN: 1-59200-862-3
Price: $24.99 US; $33.95 CDN
Page count: 304

WEIGHT TRAINING

MARAN ILLUSTRATED™ Weight Training is an information-packed guide that covers all the basics of weight training, as well as more advanced techniques and exercises.

MARAN ILLUSTRATED™ Weight Training contains more than 500 full-color photographs of exercises for every major muscle group, along with clear, step-by-step instructions for performing the exercises. Useful tips provide additional information and advice to help enhance your weight training experience.

MARAN ILLUSTRATED™ Weight Training provides all the information you need to start weight training or to refresh your technique if you have been weight training for some time.

ISBN: 1-59200-866-6
Price: $24.99 US; $33.95 CDN
Page count: 320

YOGA

MARAN ILLUSTRATED™ Yoga provides a wealth of simplified, easy-to-follow information about the increasingly popular practice of Yoga. This easy-to-use guide is a must for visual learners who prefer to see and do without having to read lengthy explanations.

Using clear, step-by-step instructions accompanied by over 500 full-color photographs, this book includes all the information you need to get started with yoga or to enhance your technique if you have already made yoga a part of your life. MARAN ILLUSTRATED™ Yoga shows you how to safely and effectively perform a variety of yoga poses at various skill levels, how to breathe more efficiently, how to customize your yoga practice to meet your needs and much more.

ISBN: 1-59200-868-2
Price: $24.99 US; $33.95 CDN
Page count: 320

Did you like this book? MARAN ILLUSTRATED™ offers books on the most popular computer topics, using the same easy-to-use format of this book. We always say that if you like one of our books, you'll love the rest of our books too!

Here's a list of some of our best-selling computer titles:

Guided Tour Series - 240 pages, Full Color

MARAN ILLUSTRATED's Guided Tour series features a friendly disk character that walks you through each task step by step. The full-color screen shots are larger than in any of our other series and are accompanied by clear, concise instructions.

	ISBN	Price
MARAN ILLUSTRATED™ Computers Guided Tour	1-59200-880-1	$24.99 US/$33.95 CDN
MARAN ILLUSTRATED™ Windows XP Guided Tour	1-59200-886-0	$24.99 US/$33.95 CDN

MARAN ILLUSTRATED™ Series - 320 pages, Full Color

This series covers 30% more content than our Guided Tour series. Learn new software fast using our step-by-step approach and easy-to-understand text. Learning programs has never been this easy!

	ISBN	Price
MARAN ILLUSTRATED™ Windows XP	1-59200-870-4	$24.99 US/$33.95 CDN
MARAN ILLUSTRATED™ Office 2003	1-59200-890-9	$29.99 US/$40.95 CDN
MARAN ILLUSTRATED™ Excel 2003	1-59200-876-3	$24.99 US/$33.95 CDN
MARAN ILLUSTRATED™ Access 2003	1-59200-872-0	$24.99 US/$33.95 CDN

101 Hot Tips Series - 240 pages, Full Color

Progress beyond the basics with MARAN ILLUSTRATED's 101 Hot Tips series. This series features 101 of the coolest shortcuts, tricks and tips that will help you work faster and easier.

	ISBN	Price
MARAN ILLUSTRATED™ Windows XP 101 Hot Tips	1-59200-882-8	$19.99 US/$26.95 CDN